EDITOR Sara M. Gardner
DESIGN & ILLUSTRATIONS Maya Bank
CHAIR, ORGANIZING COMMITTEE Margarita Gokun Silver
PROJECT MANAGER Yael Cobano

Publisher CreateSpace
Printed in the United States

Copyright © 2018, 2019 Reform Jewish Community of Madrid
(Comunidad Judía Reformista de Madrid)
Photographs © Sara M. Gardner
Illustrations © Maya Bank

All rights reserved.
ISBN: 1722239123
ISBN-13: 978-1722239121

*To our matriarchs: Sara, Rebecca, Rachel, and Leah.
And to mine: Sarah, Selma, Madeleine, and Marci.*

CONTENTS

10 ## Introduction

- 12   *Letter from the President*
- 14   *About the Rosh Hashanah Seder*
- 18   *How to Lead a Rosh Hashanah Seder*

22 ## Recipes

24 ### APPLE

- 27   *Salad Olivier, or Ensaladilla Rusa*
- 29   *Ilana's Tsimmes*
- 30   *Duck Breast with Apples, Cranberries, & Mint*
- 32   *Apple Strudel*
- 35   *Silka's Apple Cake*
- 36   *Classic Apple Crumble*

38 ### BEANS

- 41   *Turkish Bean Salad*
- 42   *Leidy's Beans with Ground Beef*
- 44   *Sara's Black Beans*
- 46   *Dani's Cocido*
- 48   *Zohar's White Beans with Honey*
- 50   *Green Bean Esparragados*

52 ### BEET

- 55   *Margarita's Beet and Apple Salad*
- 57   *The Stayermans' Borscht*
- 58   *Beet Waldorf Salad*
- 61   *Meme's Beet and Apple Salad*
- 63   *Margarita's Svekol'nik*
- 64   *Beet and Lentil "Burgers"*

66 DATE

- 69   Middle Eastern Carrot Salad
- 71   Ilana's Date, Apricot, Rice Salad
- 72   Fried Eggplant with Date Syrup
- 75   Alicia's Holiday Chicken with Dried Fruit
- 76   Date Walnut Pie
- 79   Date Pudding Cake
- 80   Date Truffles

82 FISH

- 84   Orange Salmon
- 85   Margarita's Forshmak
- 87   Ceutan Fish (Fish with Pipirrana)
- 89   Alicia's Soy-Silan Salmon
- 90   Yael's Sabbath Cod Fritters
- 92   Guefilte Fish

94 HONEY

- 96   Alicia's Challah
- 98   Honeyed Turnips
- 99   Honey Chicken
- 101   Turkish Poppy Seed Cake
- 102   Yael's Honey Cigars

104   LEEK

106	Noa's Leek Salad
107	Adele's Leek Crema
109	Roasted Leeks with Balsamic Reduction & Goat Cheese
110	Borekas de Prasa
112	Leek Kofte
114	Pasta with Leek Sauce and Salmon

116   POMEGRANATE

119	Festive Pomegranate Salad
120	Pomegranate Gazpacho
123	Quinoa Salad with Pomegranate, Orange, & Watercress
125	Marisa's Jewelled Rice
126	The Israeli Ambassador's Cauliflower
129	Pomegranate Steak

130   SQUASH

133	Italian Cream of Pumpkin Soup
135	Margarita's Squash Fritters
136	Marisa's Squash Empanadillas
138	Emanuele's Squash Galette
140	The Stayerman's Creamy Squash Soup
141	Squash and Sage Pie
143	Roasted Squash with Walnut Arugula Sauce

144 MENUS

146 *Autumn Seasonal*

147 *Summer Seasonal*

148 *Spanish*

149 *Sweet Seder*

150 *Ottoman Sephardic*

151 *Comunidad Special*

152 *Mediterranean*

153 *Ashkenazi-inspired*

154 *Israeli-inspired*

155 *Hors D'Oeuvres*

Acknowledgements

The making of this book was truly the work of community. Represented in its pages are not only the flavors and stories that make up the vibrant Reform Jewish Community of Madrid, but also the hours, weeks, and months of work that members of the community willingly donated to bring this book to life. We have a long list of people to acknowledge for helping us to turn this dream into a hardbound book.

First and foremost, I want to thank Yael Cobano. It is because of Yael that I can call the Reform Jewish Community my spiritual home in Madrid and I can pinpoint the origin of this project. This book formed over one of our long, laugh-filled telephone conversations, with me in my parents' house in Connecticut and Yael in her Madrid apartment. Despite the distance between us over this past year, those conversations were the fuel that made this project happen. From when we first starting toying with the idea of writing a cookbook until now, you have been an essential partner in making this book a reality. I am always grateful for your friendship and the inspiration it provides me – I only hope that I inspire you the same.

I also want to express my deep gratitude to Margarita Gokun Silver, who lent her vision, her passion, and her brilliance to this project. There were many moments where we found ourselves paralyzed, without a clear plan of action forward, and it was Margarita who urged us forward at every step – from orchestrating our Jewcer campaign to putting deadlines on major swaths of text, your enthusiasm and clear eyed direction was critical for this book to come to be – thank you.

I want to extend sincere thanks to Maya Bank, who was both fundamental to the planning as well as graphic elaboration of this book. Your hard work and dedication show through the coherence and beauty of these pages and I so appreciate the time you spent to so beautifully express on paper the ideas we spoke about.

Further, I want to extend my heartfelt appreciation for all the members of the Reform Jewish Community of Madrid. You all not only made this cookbook possible by sharing pieces of yourselves – your recipes and your stories – but you also will always claim a piece of my heart as my Madrid family. The year I spent living in Spain would not have been the same if it weren't for you and your weekly embrace of this *chica americana*. I hope you understand this book as my love-filled homage to you all and how much you mean to me. I also want to thank those who contributed recipes even if they didn't make into the book.

I also want to give a shout-out to my loving family – my parents, Marci Sternheim and Sam Gardner, my brothers and acquired sisters, Jake and Kate, Max and Tina, and my sweet nephew Henry – for their unyielding support. You inspire me every day to be a better person and your constant, unwavering support for my passions and projects keeps me afloat and enables me to succeed. This book, particularly the recipes that come from our family, is also a testament to you and to my love for you.

Another acknowledgement is for my best friend and roommate, Julia, who so kindly and patiently allowed me to take over and make a mess of our kitchen for so many weekends in a row. And thank you to my wonderful friends who so willingly tried these dishes and gave me their support and sincere feedback – you all helped make this process an even greater joy, bringing my Boston and Spain communities together through food.

I must also give a heartfelt *grasias* to my college advisor, Gloria Ascher, for instilling in me a deep love of the Sephardic tradition and helping me follow that passion to Spain.

Thank you to everyone who donated to our Jewcer campaign – whether it was five or five hundred dollars, every penny ensures that the Reform Jewish Community of Madrid can continue to grow and provide a Jewish home to whoever may want or need one in Madrid.

And finally, last but certainly not least, thank you dear reader for buying a copy of this book and partaking in all it has to offer – dishes, stories, and people. Books, especially cookbooks, do not exist in isolation. Their continued existence and relevance is predicated on their use; it is what keeps them alive. May this be a book that you not only sustain through its use, but also one through which you can connect and feel a part of the global Jewish community. Thank you so much for allowing us to share our stories and recipes with you.

Sara M. Gardner
Editor

Letter from the President

Just like my mother wandered around her grandmother's kitchen in Chaouen, the blue city of Morocco, so did I around my mother's kitchen in Ceuta, the Andalusian-inflected North African enclave of Spain where I was born. Within me, I carry the Judeo-Moroccan, Moroccan, and Andalusian cuisines. I observed and helped her. Ingrained in my memory are my mother's hands covered in oil to shape *sfenjs*, deep-fried donuts, or coated in butter to separate couscous grains for *cuscus con carne*, topped with meat, or *con verduras*, with vegetables. I remember the intuitive mix of spices she used to make pastries, dishes of meat or fish. After cooking, we always burned some *alhucema* – lavender – in a clay pot with alcohol to perfume the house. The smell of lavender, which I always believed to be purifying, ended up intermingling with the scent of the dishes she prepared. Today, in my apartment in Madrid, I have an entire cupboard called "the Shuk", my own little cupboard market, filled with spices, dried herbs, orange and rose waters, and lavender. I cannot live without it.

Food has always occupied a central place in my family – whether during family celebrations and festive get-togethers or simply in our daily life. Eating is our leisure activity at home and our way of learning about new places when we visit them.

It wasn't until I crossed the Strait of Gibraltar and met Jews from different countries that I began to discover a variety of Jewish cuisines, ingredients, and flavors. I often take part in verbal battles (in jest, of course) about which cuisine is better – Sephardi or Ashkenazi. I have immersed myself in the Mizrachi cuisine, that of Israel itself, and I've learned over time that many dishes of *La Peninsula* (what those of us who live on the islands or in enclaves call mainland Spain) can claim proven Jewish origin. And this way, with pride in this vibrant culinary identity, is how I take on my leadership of the Reform Jewish Community of Madrid. A community that supersedes categories and labels of merely Ashkenazi or Sephardic, it celebrates the diversity of our members and friends. Our membership hails from Venezuela, Colombia, Panama, Honduras, Turkey, Brazil, Israel, Morocco, Puerto Rico, Argentina, USA, Italy, and Spain.

This culinary diversity is reflected in our weekly table, in our holiday celebrations, in our songs, and in the very history of the *Comunidad* – the only Reform Jewish community in Spain's capital.

When Sara M. Gardner, an angel whose passion for food is as infinite as her fascination with the Jewish world and culture, joined our community, she became an integral part of it almost immediately. Hers is a wonderful example of how Jewish people – and especially young people – get involved in local communities far from their home countries. Sara helped us share our culinary traditions and educated us about their history and significance. Under her guidance Sephardim learned to cook and honor Ashkenazi dishes and vice versa. Most importantly, she taught us to love the crucible of origins which is the Jewish people. Thanks to her, we are now better acquainted with Judaism's rich textual and culinary traditions.

I'd also love to acknowledge Margarita Gokun Silver. Her love for our community inspired the idea to make a book that would share the Sephardic tradition of a Rosh Hashanah seder through the dishes of the community with the entire world. Thank you, too, to Maya Bank for contributing her stellar design skills, even from afar in Israel. And, of course, this book would never exist without our members – members of the Reform Jewish Community of Madrid – who shared their families' recipes and stories, prepared those recipes for the community, and helped us to collect them for this book.

I hope this book will help bring as many *yehi ratzones* and good omens to your Rosh Hashanah table as the dishes and histories that are encompassed in its pages. As a congregation we hope that celebrating a seder inspired by the Sephardic tradition, will bring you closer to our beautiful community in the heart of *Sepharad*. By buying this book and by preparing its recipes you're contributing to the fortification of a strong Jewish presence in a country that has given the Jewish world so many beautiful traditions and customs.

L'Shanah Tovah! May you be renewed in this new year and may you, your family, and your congregation go from strength to strength! You are always welcome to come and visit us in Madrid should your travels ever bring you to Spain.

Yael Cobano
President
Reform Jewish Community of Madrid

About the Rosh Hashanah Seder

Jewish time is replete with important and symbolic holidays. These festive days give shape to the Jewish year, orienting our intentions and spurring our communal growth with the ebb and flow of the seasons. Of all the many Jewish holidays that occur throughout the year, though, there is only one holiday that marks the new year: Rosh Hashanah.

Rosh Hashanah, literally meaning "head of the year," symbolizes the nexus between the end of one year and the beginning of the next. As it is such an important day in the Jewish calendar, so many unique rituals have been built up over time as a part of the day's celebration. Whether it's listening the blast of the *shofar* (a hollowed out ram's horn), dressing in white, or eating 12 grapes on Rosh Hashanah eve (a Cuban Jewish tradition), there are myriad ways Jewish communities all over the world mark this special holiday. Of course, these symbolic acts are not merely limited to the way Jews dress, pray, and gather; in fact, the symbolic marking of this new year's celebration is most clearly evident on the table, through the multitude of emblematic foods that global Jewish communities use to help usher in the holiday. From circular *challot* to feasts of lamb (common in Ethiopian Jewish communities) to plum tarts (a French Jewish tradition), these dishes act as the culinary ushers from the old year into the new, many of them in the process becoming the flavors that give meaning to the holiday and the transition from one year to the next.

In particular, this book focuses on one specific gastronomic tradition of Rosh Hashanah: the Sephardic Jewish Rosh Hashanah *seder*. Meaning "order" in Hebrew, the *seder* also refers to a meal with a specifically organized arc of foods and stories each food represents. The most well-known *seder* in the Jewish calendar occurs on Passover, during which global Jewish communities re-tell the story of the exodus from Egypt and eat symbol-laden foods like *matzah*, the bread of affliction; *charoset*, a fruit and nut paste or mixture that represents the bricks and mortar with which the Jews built the pyramids; and *maror*, bitter herbs that symbolizes that hardship of slavery. Yet many Sephardic communities celebrate not one, but two, yearly *seders*, including the Rosh Hashanah *seder*. At this *seder*, Sephardim (as they are also known), lay a plate full of up to nine specific ingredients, called *simanim* (signs). *Simanim* may include apples, honey, beans, beets, dates, fish heads, leeks, pomegranate, and squash. Over each of these, before the Rosh Hashanah meal begins, it is customary for Sephardic Jews to hold up each symbolic food and recite its *yehi ratzon* (also spelled *yehi ratson*), or its specific blessing, to engender certain wishes in the new year.

Practiced by Sephardic communities around the world, the Rosh Hashanah *seder* has a long precedent in the Jewish tradition, going back to the days of the Talmud. In the Babylonian Talmud, Rabbi Abaye, writing in the 5th century, responds to an exchange about Rosh Hashanah, noting "now that you said that an omen is a significant matter, a person should always be accustomed to seeing these on Rosh HaShana: Squash, and fenugreek, leeks, and dates, as each of these grows quickly and serves as a positive omen for one's actions during the coming year" (Babylonian Talmud, Horayot 12a). While both Sephardic and Ashkenazi communities prepare and eat symbolic foods, or gastronomic "omens," during the new year celebration, the tradition of making a full *seder* with the symbolic ingredients is uniquely Sephardic.

In the strict academic sense, the term "Sephardic" refers to Jews who lived in and were expelled from Spain as well as their descendants who maintain the specific religious and cultural practices of the Spanish Jewish community. Although the term now often includes the Jewish communities of the north of Africa and the Middle East, with whom Sephardim mixed communally upon their settlement there post-expulsion, it is important to note the specifically Iberian roots of the Sephardic tradition. Before the Catholic monarchs, Ferdinand and Isabel, famously expelled the Jewish community from Spain in 1492, Sephardim formed an important element of medieval Spanish society and life. In both the southern Islamic caliphates and northern Christian kingdoms of Spain, the Sephardic Jews formed an intrinsic part of the economic, social, and cultural wellbeing of medieval Spanish realms. They lived and worked as doctors, poets, translators, highly successful merchants, even viziers and advisors to kings and caliphs alike – adeptly garnering prestige that would later contribute the period's title of the Spanish Jewish Golden Age.

This prosperity of the medieval Spanish Jewish community, however, began to deteriorate at the end of the 14th century, with a wave of violent massacres that starting in Andalusia that swept up the Iberian Peninsula. These pogroms initiated a wave of Spanish Jewish migration out of Spain and across the Mediterranean, steadily increasing and finally culminating in the Catholic monarchs' 1492 expulsion of the Sephardim (coincidentally, three days before Christopher Columbus was set to sail for the New World). The expulsion its and consequent waves of emigration displaced the Sephardic Jewish community across the Mediterranean, the rest of Europe, and even to the New World. But wherever the Sephardic Jews went – and whether they resettled as still-practicing Jews or as *judeoconversos*, those who had been forcibly or voluntarily converted to Catholicism from Judaism – they brought with them their unique cultural and culinary traditions to their new homelands. Among the food-based rituals the Sephardim carried with them was their symbol-laden Rosh Hashanah *seder*.

This book draws its inspiration both from the the Rosh Hashanah seders of the olden Sephardic communities – and from the seders of the nascent Jewish communities of modern Spain. The latter is reflected in the culinary tradition of the diverse and vibrant Reform Jewish Community of Madrid. Home to community members with Sephardic and Spanish roots, it also includes members from Panama, Russia, Venezuela, Israel, Morocco, Colombia, Hungary and the United States. On Rosh Hashanah in the Reform Jewish Community of Madrid, also referred to as the Comunidad, all of our community members come together to welcome in the new year with a communal Rosh Hashanah seder. Together, we make dishes using the symbolic ingredients, eat the *simanim*, and say the *yehi ratzones*, inviting in all the best wishes and blessings for the new year.

Although the roots of the Rosh Hashanah seder can be found in the Sephardic tradition, it is our hope that you are compelled to adapt this lovely new year's practice to your family's custom, as we have in the Reform Jewish Community of Madrid. In so doing, may all your wishes for an a good, sweet, and happy new year –as is said in Ladino, *anyada buena, dulse i alegre* – come true.

How to Lead a Rosh Hashanah Seder

We would be remiss if in providing you with the recipes for a Rosh Hashanah *seder*, we did not explain how to make one. The Rosh Hashanah *seder* is a wonderful opportunity to bring your loved ones together around the table in a communal setting or at home, whether you lead the *seder* yourself or in community. It's a great way of more deeply involving your dinner guests in the new year's meal, whether that's through lighting candles or making *kiddush* – the blessing over wine— or eating challah with honey or inviting guests to read a *yehi ratzon*.

Here we provide some guidelines of how to lead your own Rosh Hashanah *seder*. Of course, these tips are just a beginning; if more ideas come to you about how to lead your own, the better! These suggestions find their root in our Talmudic tradition, in which good omens for the new year are enacted through seeing and eating various symbolic ingredients, also known as *simanim*. From these two ways of engaging with new year's omens – through sight and taste – developed two Rosh Hashanah *seder* traditions: one in which guests consume the symbolic foods and the other in which each symbolic ingredient is shown with its meaning and corresponding blessing explained. It is up to you which tradition you'd like to explore during your Rosh Hashanah meal.

Both ways of observing the Rosh Hashanah seder begin with the lighting of candles using the blessing for the High Holy Days. Next, the *kiddush* for the High Holy Days is recited. Don't forget also to recite the *shehechiyanu*, the blessing that celebrates the first time something is done in the Jewish year. Before beginning with the *seder*, the *hamotzi*, the blessing over the challah, is recited.

If you'd like, Rosh Hashanah seder plates are readily available for purchase online or at stores that sell Judaica. If you don't own a Rosh Hashanah seder plate, however, feel free to get creative: a normal plate serves as a ready substitute, as well as a collection of small bowls to hold each siman, or even multiple plates. The Rosh Hashanah *seder* is an opportunity to creatively engage with the Jewish tradition, so let your imagination run free in terms of presentation.

Generally, in the Reform Jewish Community of Madrid we like to start with the blessings over the dates and then the pomegranate, continuing with leeks, beans, beets, squash, and ending with the blessings over the apples, honey, and fish. That said, each community and family has its own order – some start with apples and honey and end the seder with fish; others begin with fish and end with pomegranate. Feel free to find the order of blessings that feels most meaningful to you. Below, we offer three different ways for incorporating the symbolic ingredients into your Rosh Hashanah meal and seder. We hope they each help you to ring in a sweet, happy, healthy, and fun new year!

Option A: If you have a Rosh Hashanah seder plate, place each symbolic ingredient on it or, if you don't have a plate, lay each ingredient on a plate or in a bowl on your Rosh Hashanah table so that all the simanim are plainly visible. That way, no matter your Rosh Hashanah menu, the symbolic ingredients will all be present at your meal. For this option, we do suggest choosing one or two dishes that incorporate the symbolic ingredients to add to your Rosh Hashanah menu.

If you are the leader, start by explaining to your guests where this tradition comes from (more information about that on page 14). Hold up each of the symbolic ingredients so that all of your guests can see it and recite its *yehi ratzon*. You can also ask your guests to volunteer to hold up the food themselves or lead the table in reciting the *yehi ratzon*.

After showing the symbolic ingredients and saying the blessings, point out the dishes you have prepared that include the *simanim* and explain the relevance of the ingredients' symbolism to your current life. For example, if you have chosen to include dishes made with pomegranate, fish, and dates, explain the relationship of these ingredients your life: perhaps you chose to include pomegranate so that your year may be as full of time with your loved ones as the pomegranate is full of seeds; the fish, to invite success in your studies in the new year, as you want to be in the head of your class and not the tail; the dates, because you are single and wish to have more dates in the new year to find your partner. Invite your guests to add their own interpretations of each siman as a part of the discussion during the meal.

Option B: If you're interested in incorporating your guests and the *simanim* more fully in your Rosh Hashanah meal and ritual, try this option.

Prepare a dish that incorporates each *siman* in the actual meal (feel free to use the recipes from this book and the menus beginning on page 144 for inspiration). Place each of the prepared dishes in the middle of your table in a circle to mimic the form of a seder plate. You can ask each guest to select a dish to bring as a part of this experience. Before eating, go around the table and explain or have the guest who prepared the dish explain why that ingredient and that dish were chosen. Recite each *yehi ratzon* together as a table after the presentation of each dish.

This option is particularly fun should you have many guests at your Rosh Hashanah seder. We encourage you, or whoever leads the seder, to invite discussion among the guests about the *simanim* and their wishes for the new year after each dish is presented.

Option C: The last option is for those who don't have much time to prepare for the seder but still want to include the *simanim* in their new year's celebration.

Feel free to select a few dishes from this book that incorporate the symbolic ingredients. Before eating, explain where the Rosh Hashanah seder tradition comes from, recite the *yehi ratzones* together, and dig into your holiday meal. This is the most straightforward option should you have limited time to prepare a seder.

Of course, all of these options are wonderful opportunities to invite questions and reflections about the old and new years from your guests. Use this *seder* as a time to connect with your loved ones, tell family stories old and new, and teach the joys of the Jewish new year. No matter how you ring in your new year, though – whether by leading a seder or simply by preparing a few special dishes – may it help you invite sweetness and blessings into your new year. *L'shanah tova umetukah*!

For more information on how to lead your Rosh Hashanah *seder* and to see how the Reform Jewish Community of Madrid leads its *seder*, feel free to view the official Rosh Hashanah Seder Cookbook Seder leading video here: https://youtu.be/B3FwU284dr8.

Recipes

24 APPLE

27	*Salad Olivier, or Ensaladilla Rusa*
29	*Ilana's Tsimmes*
30	*Duck Breast with Apples, Cranberries & Mint*
32	*Apple Strudel*
35	*Silka's Apple Cake*
36	*Classic Apple Crumble*

The apple is arguably the most familiar symbol of the Jewish year. Traditional in Ashkenazi households on Rosh Hashanah, the apple is also an important sign of renewal in the new year for Sephardic Jews. Beyond their use on Rosh Hashanah, though, apples possess a deep symbolism within the Jewish tradition – they famously appear in multiple lines of the Song of Songs as expressions of both romantic and divine love. Moreover, the rabbinic sages of the Talmud often identified the Jewish people with apple trees and the divine presence with apple orchards. In that way, when we eat apples on Rosh Hashanah, we not only entreat personal renewal in the year to come, but also a reaffirmed connection to the Jewish tradition through their inclusion in the Rosh Hashanah seder.

יְהִי רָצוֹן מִלְּפָנֶיךָ ה' אֱלֹהֵינוּ וֵאלֹהֵי אֲבוֹתֵינוּ, שֶׁתְּחַדֵּשׁ עָלֵינוּ שָׁנָה טוֹבָה וּמְתוּקָה כַּדְּבַשׁ

Yehi ratzon milfanecha Adonai eloheinu v'elohei avoteinu v'imoteinu, she't'chadesh aleinu shanah tovah u'metukah ka'devash.

May it be Your will, God and the God of our ancestors, that You renew for us a year good and sweet like honey.

Salad Olivier, or Ensaladilla Rusa

Serves 8-10.

A common tapa in Spanish bars is *ensaladilla rusa*, or Russian salad, a mixture of chopped boiled potatoes, olives, tuna, and mayonnaise. Despite its French-sounding name, it turns out that this salad is actually a classic of the Russian repertoire as well – except the Russian original swaps out the olives and tuna for grated apple, hardboiled eggs, and chopped dill pickles. Serve the salad cold or at room temperature, for a potato salad that is surprisingly addictive in any language.

Ingredients

3 medium sized waxy potatoes (such as Yukon Gold), peeled and boiled
2 medium sized carrots, peeled and boiled
1 egg, hardboiled
2 medium sized Dill pickles (we used Vlassic brand original whole Dill pickles), minced
Half a bunch of dill, chopped

Half a bunch of cilantro, stems removed and chopped
1 Granny Smith apple, peeled and chopped
½ cup mayonnaise
Salt and freshly ground black pepper to taste

Process

Chop the potatoes, carrots, and egg. Combine in a large bowl with pickles, dill, cilantro, and apple. Mix well. Add the mayonnaise and mix until well combined. Season with salt and pepper to taste.

Ilana's Tsimmes

Serves 8-10.

Tsimmes are a classic dish of the Ashkenazi (Eastern-European) Jewish repertoire. Although the Rosh Hashanah seder is a Sephardic tradition, the Reform Jewish Community of Madrid is lucky to have members of the congregation from all parts of the world and all Jewish traditions. So, it makes sense to include this comforting Ashkenazi dish that uses apples to help give the combination of carrots and prunes an extra bit of sweetness. It's a perfect side dish to a savory meat main, such as the Pomegranate Steaks, found on page 129.

Ingredients

- 3 tablespoons neutral oil, such as vegetable or canola oil
- 3 carrots, peeled and sliced 1" thick on the diagonal
- 1 very full cup of prunes, whole
- 2 apples (preferably Macintosh or Cortland), peeled, cored, and diced
- 3 tablespoons honey
- 2 cups water
- 1" piece of ginger, peeled and grated
- ½ teaspoon cardamom seeds
- 1 cinnamon stick
- Pinch of salt

Process

Heat the oil in a large skillet over medium heat. Add the carrots and cook for about 10 minutes, or until they start to soften. Add the apples, prunes, ginger, cardamom, and salt. Cook for another 5 minutes, until the apples start to soften and the spices release their fragrance.

Add the water, cinnamon stick, and honey, stirring well. Bring mixture to a boil, then turn the heat to low and let the mixture simmer, stirring occasionally, for 30 minutes, until the water has completely reduced to a syrup and the carrots are completely tender. Remove the cinnamon stick before serving.

Duck Breast with Apples, Cranberries & Mint

Serves 2.

This recipe was a special occasion dish in Margarita's family – her grandmother would make it only once a year in the former Soviet Union for New Year's Eve dinner. In its original form, a whole duck is stuffed with apples, cranberries, and mint and roasted until golden and sweet. Margarita says her family would always argue over who could eat the darker parts of the duck, which were the sweetest. In this version, we've opted to sear a duck breast, which is much easier to find and prepare than a whole duck, and serve it with a succulent sauce of cooked onions, apples, and cranberries. Although Russian and Polish in origin, this dish will surely be an appropriate addition to an autumnal Rosh Hashanah table anywhere.

Ingredients

1 pound duck breast with skin personas
1 large sweet onion, sliced
4 tablespoons olive oil
2 tablespoons sugar
2 green apples, peeled, cored, and thinly sliced
1 cup fresh or frozen cranberries
¼ cup dry red wine

Juice of half a lemon
A few sprigs of fresh mint
1 teaspoon salt
Freshly ground pepper to taste

Process

In large skillet, heat 2 tablespoons of olive oil over medium-high heat. Season the duck breast with the salt and pepper on all sides. Using a sharp paring knife, create crosshatched incisions on the skin side of the duck breast, being careful to not cut into the meat of the duck itself.

Once the pan is hot, place the duck breast(s) skin side down and sear it (them) until the fat is rendered and the skin is crisp, about 10 minutes. Turn the heat to medium-low, flip the breast(s) and cook the other side for another 6 to 8 minutes. Once the duck is cooked (it should be cooked medium rare or to an internal temperature of at least 140°F; for a more well-done breast, leave it in the pan on medium-low for a few minutes more, or until the internal temperature of the duck is 160°F), remove it from the pan and set it on a cutting board to rest. Discard all of the rendered fat except for 3 tablespoons.

Once the duck is removed from the pan, re-heat 3 tablespoons of the rendered duck fat over medium heat. Add the onion and cook, stirring frequently, until the onions start to turn golden, about 12-15 minutes. Mix the sugar and a pinch of salt into the onions. Cook for another minute or so, until the sugar dissolves into the onions. Add the cranberries and the apples, and sauté them until they start to release their juice, about 3 minutes. Add ¼ cup of water, the red wine, and the lemon juice. Stir well to combine.

Cook the mixture over medium heat, stirring occasionally, for another 12 to 15 minutes, until the sauce thickens and the fruit starts to cook down. Five minutes before you take the sauce off of the flame, add a sprig or two of mint. Once the sauce is thickened, remove the pan from the heat and set aside.

To serve, cut the duck breast in ¼-inch slices. Place on top or alongside of the apple-cranberry sauce. Garnish with more mint.

Apple Strudel

Serves 6-8.

Apple strudel is traditionally made by rolling a mix of apples, cinnamon, and sugar in a paper-thin sheet of phyllo dough, which is then brushed with butter and baked until golden brown. This version, contributed by a community member who learned how to make it in a Spanish cooking course, is a very Spanish interpretation of the classic dessert. Instead of using thin, crispy phyllo, this recipe uses a type of cake that has a sponge-like consistency with which to roll up grated apples. It is reminiscent of another common Spanish dessert called (perhaps now somewhat controversially) *brazo de gitano*, or a gypsey's arm cake. In Spain, *brazos de gitano* are usually filled with pastry cream and covered in chocolate – they are quite delicious, although this Spanish version of strudel makes for a much more appropriate addition to the Rosh Hashanah dessert table.

Ingredients

For the dough:

2 tablespoons vegetable oil or melted butter
6 eggs, separated
¾ cup flour, plus more for dusting
¾ cup sugar
1 teaspoon vanilla extract
Pinch of salt

For the filling:

5 apples (preferably Granny Smith) peeled cored, and grated
3/4 cup sugar
1 teaspoon ground cinnamon
Juice of half a lemon
¾ cup raisins
½ cup chopped walnuts

Process

To make the filling: Mix the grated apples with the sugar, cinnamon, lemon juice, raisins, and walnuts. Stir to combine. Set aside.

To make the dough: Preheat the oven to 425°F. In a bowl, beat the 6 egg yolks with the sugar until creamy and pale yellow, 3 to 5 minutes. Mix in the flour and vanilla until well-combined. In a separate clean bowl, beat the egg whites with an electric mixer until they form soft peaks. Fold the beaten egg whites delicately into the egg yolk and flour mixture until well combined.

Make the strudel: Line a baking sheet with parchment paper. Lightly grease the parchment paper with the oil. Turn the dough out onto the baking sheet and spread the dough evenly over the parchment paper. Bake about 4 to 6 minutes, or until evenly golden brown and a cake tester inserted in the center comes out clean. Let cool for 5 minutes, so it can be handled.

Spread the filling evenly over the dough, leaving an inch of dough uncovered on the short edges. Using the parchment paper to turn the dough, roll the short edge of the dough, continuously peeling off the parchment paper, until you've created a jelly roll-like log. Serve immediately in thick slices with whipped cream.

Silka's Apple Cake

Serves 8-10.

This recipe was given to a community member by an Israeli woman named Silka, who lived on a kibbutz in Israel for many years before moving to Madrid. Although this is the recipe of an Israeli woman, the technique of using a yogurt cup as the measuring implement to make a delicious cake is very common in Spain. In that way, this recipe reflects both the Israeli and Spanish roots of this apple cake, symbolic of the diverse origins of the Reform Jewish Community of Madrid.

Ingredients

- 6 ounce cup of plain yogurt
- 3 apples (preferably Macintosh or Granny Smith), unpeeled, cored, and diced
- 1 ½ yogurt cups (1 ¼ cup) brown sugar, loosely packed
- 3 yogurt cups (2 ¼ cups flour)
- 1 yogurt cup (3/4 cup) olive oil
- 2 eggs
- 2 teapoons baking powder
- 1 teaspoon of cinnamon
- 1 teaspoon vanilla
- ¼ cup milk
- Pinch salt
- Confectioner's sugar, for dusting

Process

Preheat the oven to 350°F. Grease a 10" springform pan with a tablespoon of olive oil.

In a large bowl, mix the yogurt, olive oil, eggs, milk, and vanilla. In another large bowl, whisk together the sugar, flour, baking powder, cinnamon, and the salt. Pour the wet ingredients into the dry and mix together thoroughly. Add the diced apples and mix until just combined.

Pour batter into pre-greased springform. Bake for 50-55 minutes, or until a cake tester inserted into the center of the cake comes out clean. Let cool 10 minutes then remove from the springform pan. Dust with confectioner's sugar before serving.

Classic Apple Crumble

Serves 6-8.

Arielle adapted this recipe, an American classic, from *The New York Times*. Crumbles, crisps, and the whole genre of crumb-topped fruit desserts is generally unknown to the Spanish kitchen, although it's well-loved in the United States. In that way, aside from offering a sweet and very easy to prepare finish to your Rosh Hashanah meal, this dessert also symbolizes the delicious outcomes that occur when we share our holiday tastes and traditions.

Ingredients

1 ½ sticks (12 tablespoons) cold unsalted butter, cubed, plus a little bit to grease the pan
1 ½ cup flour
1 ½ cup brown sugar
1 cup rolled oats
1 cup walnuts, chopped

8 Granny Smith apples, peeled, cored, and sliced
1 tablespoon ground cinnamon
2 tablespoons lemon juice
Pinch of salt

Process

Preheat the oven to 350°F. Butter a 13" by 9" baking pan or Pyrex dish.

In a large bowl, combine the flour, 1 cup of the brown sugar, the rolled oats and walnuts. Add the butter and mix into the flour mixture with your hands or a fork until it is evenly distributed and forms pea-sized lumps.

In another bowl, mix the apple slices with the remaining ½ cup of brown sugar, the cinnamon, lemon juice, and salt. Pour the apples and spread evenly in the baking dish. Top with the flour-sugar-butter mixture, taking handfuls of the mixture and pressing them with your hand to form clumps. Place in the preheated oven and bake for 50 to 60 minutes, or until the topping is golden brown and the apples are softened. Serve warm or at room temperature, preferably with a nice dollop of whipped cream.

38 BEANS

41	*Margarita's Turkish Bean Salad*
42	*Leidy's Beans with Ground Beef*
44	*Sara's Famous Black Beans*
46	*Dani's Cocido*
48	*Zohar's White Beans with Honey*
50	*Green Beans Esparragados*

In Spanish and in Ladino, the Judeo-Spanish language of the Sephardic Jews, there are many words for beans depending on the type of bean you're looking for. If you want the dried, kidney-shaped kind of beans, you would ask for *alubias*, *habas*, or *habichuelas* in Spanish or *avas* or *abas* in Ladino. In English, however, beans can include the long pods that beans come in as well as the small seeds within them. In Ladino, the word for string beans is *fasulyas*. Interestingly, the Spanish word for green beans is *judia*, very close to the Spanish word for "Jew" or "Jewish," which is *judía*. Simply by adding the accent, the word goes from meaning green bean to Jew(ish). Just as beans have many linguistic derivations, so, too, do they symbolize the variety of good wishes in the new year, since their Aramaic word, *rubiya*, plays on the Hebrew words for "many" – *rav* – and "heart" – *lev*. May their inclusion on your Rosh Hashanah table bring you an abundance of blessings in the new year!

יְהִי רָצוֹן מִלְּפָנֶיךָ ה' אֱלֹהֵינוּ וֵאלֹהֵי אֲבוֹתֵינוּ וְאִימוֹתֵינוּ, שֶׁיִּרְבּוּ זְכִיּוֹתֵינוּ וּתְלַבְּבֵנוּ

Yehi ratzon milfanecha Adonai eloheinu v'elohei avoteinu v'imoteinu she'yirbu zakiyoteinu u't'leivavenu.

May it be Your will, God and the God of our ancestors, that our merits shall increase and that You hearten us.

Margarita's Turkish Bean Salad

Serves 2 for a light lunch, or 4 as a side dish.

Margarita adapted this bean recipe from a Turkish one she found by adding the cilantro and feta cheese. Particularly if Rosh Hashanah has arrived in early September, this salad can take advantage of summer's last ripe tomatoes to include as a part of your abundant holiday table.

Ingredients

1 can red kidney beans
2 medium, very ripe tomatoes, diced
1 loose cup chopped parsley or cilantro
½ yellow bell pepper, diced
½ red bell pepper, diced
8 oz. feta cheese, diced
¼ cup extra virgin olive oil
Juice of ½ lemon
Salt and black pepper to taste

Process

In a large mixing bowl, combine the beans, tomatoes, parsley or cilantro, peppers, and feta cheese. Dress with the olive oil and lemon juice and season with salt and pepper to taste.

Leidy's Beans with Ground Beef

Serves 4.

Leidy tells of the familiarity of this dish, explaining that *for me, this dish recalls my childhood in Colombia. My mother prepared it nearly every Saturday. The only difference in the way I make this dish from how my mother made it is that I add the ground meat. Now it's my kids' favorite Sabbath dish in the fall and winter. They love it and it's their comfort food, now that my eldest daughter lives in Israel, my son lives on his own, and my youngest daughter is at college.* Just as this dish brings together Leidy's family from near and far, may it also serve to join the ones dearest to you around the Rosh Hashanah table.

Ingredients

11 oz. pinto beans, soaked overnight
3 cloves of garlic, skin removed
2 onions, finely chopped, separated
1 bay leaf
½ teaspoon paprika
½ teaspoon brown sugar
1 ½ cups canned crushed tomatoes
6 tablespoons olive oil
1 teaspoon ground cumin
1 teaspoon salt
1 cup chopped cilantro
½ pound ground veal or ground beef (20% fat)

Process

Drain the soaked beans. Place them in a large 4 quart saucepan with the garlic cloves and bay leaf, and cover them with 6 cups of water. Heat over medium and cook the beans until they are soft enough to be crushed with a fork but don't disintegrate. Take them off the heat and set aside, separating them from the cooking liquid but reserving the liquid for later.

Meanwhile, in a pan over medium-high heat, heat 3 tablespoons of olive oil. Sauté one of the chopped onions until it turns golden brown, about 10 minutes, then add the crushed tomatoes, sugar, paprika, and ½ teaspoon of salt. Add the beans and a ½ cup of their cooking liquid to the mixture and cook them over medium heat another 15 minutes, or until the liquid is slightly reduced.

In another pan, heat the other 3 tablespoons of olive oil over medium-high heat. Add the remaining chopped onion and sauté until it begins to brown, about 5 to 7 minutes. Add the ground meat, the cumin, ground black pepper, and the remaining ½ teaspoon of salt. Cook until the meat is completely cooked through, about ten minutes, stirring frequently to break up the meat thoroughly. Once the meat is cooked through, add it to the beans while still on the heat. Mix well and add the cilantro. When everything is well mixed, take it off the heat and serve over rice.

Sara's Famous Black Beans

Serves 4-6.

I'm not sure where exactly this recipe came from, but I started making these black beans in college, improvising and improving the recipe as I went. I knew it was a winner when my discerning older brother, Max, asked me to show him how to make them. These beans are a regular staple for dinner in my house, and now his as well. I've found that the key to making really delicious beans is letting each ingredient that's added to the pan have its time to cook and impart its flavor to the dish. These beans great for any night of the week, served over white rice and topped with sliced avocado and an extra squeeze of lime, but can give your Rosh Hashanah meal an unexpected, tasty Tex-Mex twist.

Ingredients

3 tablespoons olive oil
1 large onion, halved and thinly sliced
3 cloves garlic, minced
1 jalapeño, seeds removed from half and finely minced (optional)
1 1 lb 13 oz can of black beans, drained and rinsed
3 tablespoons tomato paste
1 bunch cilantro, chopped
1 teaspoon cumin
1 teaspoon dried oregano
½ teaspoon cayenne pepper
¼ teaspoon ground cinnamon
½ teaspoon paprika
1 teaspoon salt
½ teaspoon freshly ground black pepper
1 bay leaf
1 ½ cups water
Juice of 1 lime

Process

Heat the oil in a large skillet over medium-high heat. Once the oil is hot, add the onion and cook for 10 minutes, or until softened and starting to caramelize. Add the garlic and jalapeño (if using) and cook, stirring frequently for 3 minutes, or until fragrant. Add the drained beans, and stir to combine, cooking 2 minutes.

Make a small well in the middle of the beans and aromatics. Place the tomato paste there and let cook for 30 seconds before stirring to coat the other ingredients. Cook the tomato-paste-coated beans for another 2 minutes. Make another well and add

the cumin, oregano, cayenne pepper, cinnamon, and paprika. Let the spices toast for 30 seconds then stir them in to coat the beans. Cook for another 2 minutes. Stir in the cilantro and continue cooking, about 2 more minutes.

Stir in the salt, pepper, bay leaf. Add the water and lime juice and stir to combine. Bring the mixture to a boil and then turn down to a simmer. Let the beans simmer for 20 minutes, or until the liquid has reduced and the beans are very soft. Serve over white rice with an extra lime wedge and accompanied by sliced avocado.

Dani's Cocido

Serves 10-12.

Cocido is a well-known and well-loved dish across Spain. A soup made of a grand mixture of various types of meats (most often pork products including ham, *chorizo*, pork chops, as well as beef and a full chicken), *cocido* has been in the Spanish culinary repertoire for centuries. In fact, this specific recipe for *cocido* comes from a community member whose ancestors, from a small town in the province of Toledo, converted to Catholicism centuries ago during the period of religious turmoil that culminated in the Catholic Monarchs' expulsion of the Sephardic Jews from Spain in 1492. Dani's ancestors, like so many other medieval Spanish Jews who were forcibly or voluntarily converted from Judaism to Catholicism, continued to express their Jewish identity in many ways. In addition to having to memorize the last names of those families that his parents told him were *de los nuestros* ("of our own") and of *la misma pelaje* ("the same skin"), Dani recalls that his mother learned how to make this cocido, conspicuously absent of pork products or any other non-kosher meats, from her grandmothers, who learned it from their grandmothers. Make this lamb *cocido* for your Rosh Hashanah *seder*, and you'll not only be connected to the Sephardic tradition but also to the tradition of those crypto-Jews ("secret"- Jews) and *judeoconversos* (Judeoconverts) who adapted classic Spanish Christian dishes to their Jewish practices. It's a remarkable culinary symbol of Jewish continuity and solidarity in the face of incredible odds.

Ingredients

11 oz. dried garbanzo beans
1 ½ pounds lamb leg, shoulder, or breast or beef brisket
Enough cold water to cover the meats, plus 1 ½ cups
1 lamb or beef bone (with marrow if you'd like a more gelatinous soup)
¾ pound chicken thighs
6 medium waxy potatoes, skin left on
5 medium carrots, peeled, cut into 1-inch chunks
1 pound green beans, cut into 2-inch pieces
1 pound butternut squash or sweet potatoes, peeled and cut into 1-inch chunks
8 oz or 1 bunch green Swiss chard ripped into 1-inch pieces
½ pound white cabbage, sliced in ½-inch pieces
1 large or 3 medium leeks, cut in 1 inch pieces
1 – 2 tablespoons of salt (enough to taste)
1 bunch of mint (preferably hierbuena or spearmint) or a small handful fresh thyme

Process

The night before preparing the *cocido*, set the garbanzo beans in a bowl with enough water to cover to soak overnight. Before making the cocido, drain and rinse the garbanzos. Set aside until use.

In a large pot (at least 10 inches wide and 8 inches deep), place the lamb or brisket, chicken thighs, and the marrow bone, if using. Fill the pot with enough cold water to cover all the meats, and then add the 1 ½ cups extra water and a tablespoon of salt. Heat the pot over the highest heat and bring to a boil. Boil the mixture for 10-15 minutes. Once the mixture starts to boil, add the soaked and rinsed garbanzos. You will start to see a foam forming at the tops and edges of the pot. Using a wooden or metal spoon, remove the foam from the boiling liquid and discard. Every time you add new ingredients, the foam will reappear; every time this happens simply use a spoon to remove the foam and discard it. As the mixture boils, the liquid will begin to evaporate; keep adding water in ½ cup increments to maintain the original level of liquid in the soup.

After boiling the mixture and removing the foam for 10-15 minutes, lower the heat to medium-low, and simmer the soup, partially covered for two to two-and-half hours, or until the garbanzos are tender. (You should be able to easily crush them with a fork.) Over this time, check the mixture every 20 minutes or so to continue adding water in increments of ½ cup and removing any foam that appears. Stir occasionally as well.

Once the garbanzos are tender, add the rest of the vegetables, ending with the squash or sweet potatoes and regular potatoes. As before, add more water in ½ cup increments should the liquid be diminished. Add more salt to taste. Simmer the mixture, maintaining the simmer at medium-low heat, for another 5 minutes, then add the mint. Simmer for 10 minutes more. Remove the mixture from the heat and let cool for 5 to 10 minutes.

Before serving, take out the meat and cut or shred it into bite-sized pieces. Keep or discard the bones as you like. To serve, ladle bowlfuls of the broth and add the meat and vegetables. Eat the *cocido* as you would a soup, with plenty of crusty bread for dipping in the broth.

Zohar's White Beans with Honey

Serves 4-6.

This dish speaks to the Hungarian roots of its author with the addition of the paprika, the most treasured of Hungarian spices. It's especially delicious when made with Cannellini beans, which cook to creamy tenderness saturated in this honey-enriched sauce. Zohar notes that this dish is even more delicious when one adds spicy paprika to the cooking liquid; that being said, should you desire a more mild flavor, feel free to use sweet paprika or a combination of the two. Try to find a Hungarian variety of paprika – look for sweet *csemege* paprika or the spicy *csipős* paprika. It's up to you how much heat you'd like to bring to your Rosh Hashanah meal!

Ingredients

- 1 lb. white beans (such as Cannellini, Great Northern, Navy, or Baby Lima beans)
- 4 tablespoons of olive oil
- 2 onions, finely chopped
- 2 tablespoons of honey
- 1 tablespoon dried ground cilantro
- 1 cup crushed canned tomatoes
- 1 tablespoon tomato paste
- 2 tablespoons paprika, sweet or spicy or a combination
- 1 teaspoon of salt
- ½ teaspoon freshly ground black pepper
- 4 cups of water
- Chopped parsley or cilantro, for garnish (optional)

Process

The night before preparing the dish, prepare the beans by placing them in a heatproof bowl. Bowl 6 cups of water and pour it over the beans. Let them soak in the water overnight.

The next day, drain the beans and rinse them well. In a large pot, cover the beans in cold water and bring the mixture to a boil. Cook the beans at a consistent boil for 10-15 minutes, or until foam starts to form at the top and edges of the pot. Once the foam appears, take the beans off the heat and drain them.

Meanwhile, heat 1 tablespoon of olive oil in a shallow pan. Add the onions and sauté them until they start to turn golden, but don't burn, about 7 to 10 minutes. Remove from heat.

Then, in a large pot, add the remaining olive oil, the sautéed onion, the cooked beans, the crushed tomatoes, tomato paste, honey, salt and pepper. Stir well to mix then add the water. Cook the mixture over low heat for an hour, stirring frequently, until the beans are tender and the sauce is reduced but still liquid. If the mixture dries out too much as it cooks, gradually add more water to the mixture in ½ cup increments.

Once the beans are cooked, serve them warm over couscous, rice, or on their own, garnished with chopped cilantro or parsley.

Green Beans Esparragados

Serves 4.

This dish also goes by "Green Beans Tagine" because it is customarily prepared in a *tagine*, a ceramic vessel with a conical lid that is common in the north of Africa, from where this dish and its author hails. If you happen to have a tagine or another ceramic pot in your kitchen, I suggest you try making this recipe in it – the ceramic vessel adds something to the flavor of this dish that non-ceramic pans do not; however, don't worry if you don't own any ceramic cookware, this dish will still taste wonderful! That being said, for those who don't own a *tagine*, the title *esparragados* comes from the technique used in the recipe, *esparragar*, which refers to the method of creating a paste of bread and garlic friend in olive oil and smothering any vegetable you choose – in this case, string beans – in it to cook. This dish and its many names symbolize the connections between the south of Spain and Morocco, which is how it came to be part of the culinary repertoire of the family of the community member who contributed it to this book.

Ingredients

1 ½ pounds string beans or haricots verts
6 ounces of crusty bread, cut into thin slices
5 garlic cloves, peeled
½ teaspoon cumin seeds
1 tablespoon paprika, spicy or sweet
1 tablespoon red wine vinegar
8 tablespons olive oil
½ teaspoon salt

Process

Clean the beans and cut off the tips. In a large pot, boil water seasoned with 1 teaspoon of salt. Once it boils, add the beans and boil them for 3 to 5 minutes, or until they are *al dente*, or tender but are still slightly firm in the middle. Drain the beans, reserving 1 cup of the cooking liquid.

Meanwhile, in a pan, heat 4 tablespoons of the olive oil over medium-high. Add the slices of bread and the garlic cloves. Sauté the garlic and toast the bread, stirring frequently so all sides of the bread are coated in the olive oil, until they are golden brown. Remove the pan from the heat, taking the bread and garlic out of the pan, but keeping the oil in it. Once the bread and garlic are removed from the pan, add the paprika, and toast it in the still-warm oil, about a minute or so (until you can smell it).

In a mortar or in a food processor, place the bread and the garlic with the leftover oil from the pan and the paprika, ½ teaspoon of salt, and the cumin seeds. Mash with the pestle or pulse in the food processor. Add water, ¼ cup at a time, until a thick paste forms (you should only need about ¼ cup or so).

After you've prepared the bread mixture, heat the remaining olive oil in a skillet over medium heat. Once the oil is hot, add the beans and the bread paste to the pan and stir to coat the beans well. Turn the heat to high and add the reserved cooking liquid to the pan and the vinegar. Bring the mixture just to a boil and turn down to medium-low to simmer, cooking the beans for another 5 minutes or so, or until they are fork tender and taken on the flavor of the bread mixture.

52 BEET

55   *Margarita's Beet and Apple Salad*

57   *The Stayermans' Borscht*

58   *Beet Waldorf Salad*

61   *Meme's Beet and Apple Salad*

63   *Cold Beet Soup (Svekol'nik)*

64   *Beet and Lentil "Burgers"*

Beets may seem like an unusual addition to the Rosh Hashanah table, but in actuality this vibrant root vegetable has long been a part of the Jewish culinary tradition. In particular, it was the leaves of the beet, called *selek* or *silka* in the Talmud (these terms also denote what we now call chard), that had particular significance to the rabbinic sages in the Talmud, in part because it was considered an aphrodisiac. Of particular relevance to Rosh Hashanah is that the word *selek* is similar to the term *yistaklu*, which means to banish. Therefore, when we eat the beetroots, in addition to their greens, on Rosh Hashanah, we hope that our enemies may be banished in the new year. Due to the beet green's aphrodisiacal qualities, though, its presence on your Rosh Hashanah table will hopefully get rid of your enemies at the same time that it brings abundant love into your new year.

יְהִי רָצוֹן מִלְפָנֶיךָ ה' אֱלֹהֵינוּ וֵאלֹהֵי אֲבוֹתֵינוּ וְאִימּוֹתֵינוּ, שֶׁיִּסְתַּלְּקוּ אוֹיְבֵינוּ וְשׂוֹנְאֵינוּ וְכָל מְבַקְשֵׁי רָעָתֵנוּ

Yehi ratzon milfanecha Adonai eloheinu v'elohei avoteinu v'imoteinu, she'yistalku oyveinu v'soneinu v'kol m'vakshei ra'ateinu.

May it be Your will, God and the God of our ancestors, that our enemies, haters and those who wish evil upon us shall depart.

Margarita's Beet and Apple Salad

Serves 4.

Margarita tried this salad for the first time at a picnic with friends in Retiro, the main public park in Madrid that once was the refuge of the Spanish monarchs. She fell in love with the combination of apples and feta with the beets, which was unusual for her even though due to her family's Russian roots beet salads were commonplace. I've further adapted this salad in terms of presentation, by layering thin slices of apples and multicolored beets and topping it with the crumbled feta and almonds. Add a pinch of cayenne pepper for a touch of spiciness to complement the sweetness of the apples and beets.

Ingredients

2 medium beets, roasted and peeled (we recommend mixing colors)
1 Granny Smith apple
6 ounces feta cheese, crumbled
½ cup slivered and toasted almonds
Handful cilantro or parsley, chopped
¼ cup olive oil
½ lemon, juiced
Salt and freshly ground black pepper, to taste
Pinch of cayenne pepper (optional)

Process

Slice the beets crosswise in 1/8" slices. Slice the apple – start by placing the apple vertically on the cutting board and slice down the length of the apple, just off the side of the core. Thinly slice to create circular slices of apple, also about 1/8" thick. Repeat on the opposite side of the core, then cut the remaining sides off the apple, and slice those pieces thinly too. Set the apple slices aside and sprinkle with some of the lemon juice.

Lay the slices of beet and apple on a large plate, alternating slices of beet and apple. Sprinkle the crumbled feta, almonds, and chopped cilantro or parsley atop the beet and apple slices. Drizzle with olive and lemon juice, then season with salt, pepper, and cayenne, if using.

The Stayermans' Borscht

Serves 8-10.

This very international borscht recipe comes from a community member's mother, who received it from her mother-in-law, who learned it from her mother. This recipe has survived over generations, emigrating from Greece to South America with her family, passing through Cuba and Honduras, as they fled the wreckage of the Greco-Turkish War just before 1920. The recipe took on the flavors of Honduras, where her family eventually settled, as the addition of white rice demonstrates, and then found a new home with the Reform Jewish Commmunity of Madrid.

Ingredients

3 tablespoons olive oil
5 beets, roasted, peeled and cubed
¼ of an onion, finely chopped
½ green Italian pepper, diced
1 clove garlic, minced
5 cups water
½ cup canned crushed tomato
1 teaspoon salt

2 tablespoons sugar
½ teaspoon oregano (optional)
Heavy cream, optional
White rice, for serving

Process

Heat the olive oil in a 4-quart saucepan over medium heat. Add the onion and sauté until it becomes transparent, about 5-7 minutes. Add the garlic and continue to cook, stirring occasionally, until the garlic becomes fragrant, about 2-3 minutes. Add the peppers and continue to cook for 5 minutes. Add the beets and sauté until heated through, about 2-3 minutes.

 Add the water, crushed tomato, salt, sugar, and oregano if using Bring mixture to a boil and boil for 5 minutes, then lower to a simmer for 20 minutes. Serve hot over white rice with a touch of cream.

Beet Waldorf Salad

Serves 2-4.

The Waldorf salad is a classic salad in the United States, dating back to the late 19th century from the Waldorf-Astoria Hotel in New York City. The original salad was a mix of apples, grapes, toasted walnuts, and celery tossed in a mayonnaise dressing. This version updates this classic salad with the addition of beets, a perfect, easy-to-throw together salad for your Rosh Hashanah seder.

Ingredients

3 beets, roasted, peeled, and grated
½ cup chopped walnuts
½ cup raisins
1/3 cup mayonnaise
½ teaspoon salt
3 scallions, white and light green parts sliced

Process

In a large bowl, mix everything together. Serve topped with scallions sprinkled on top.

Meme's Beet and Apple Salad

Serves 4-6.

This is a particularly beloved salad that graces the Comunidad's Shabbat potluck dinner table every Friday. Sweet, crunchy, and juicy all at once, it combines all the best features of its ingredients. It also captures the Venezuelan roots of its creator, Meme, through the inclusion of lime and cilantro to enliven and dress the salad. On the Rosh Hashanah table, it helps to capture the seasonal aspect of the holiday, as it edibly marks the changing of summer into autumn.

Ingredients

3 beets, roasted, peeled, and diced
3 apples (preferably Golden Delicious or Granny Smith), peeled and diced
3 large tomatoes (preferably beefsteak or Brandywine), diced
1 shallot, minced
3 ribs of celery, thinly sliced (optional)

Handful of cilantro, chopped
½ teaspoon salt
Freshly ground black pepper to taste
1 tablespoon sugar
4 tablespoons olive oil
Juice of a lime

Process

In a large bowl, mix together the beets, apples, tomatoes, shallot, and celery, if using. In a small bowl, whisk together the olive oil, lime juice, salt, black pepper, sugar, and cilantro.

Dress the beet-tomato mixture with the lime-cilantro dressing and toss well to coat.

Cold Beet Soup (Svekol'nik)

Serves 8-10.

This beet soup recipe is a traditional Russian staple of community member's Margarita's household. She says that growing up in the USSR, her mother would boil beets to make this refreshing broth for the summer. Feel free to grate the boiled beets into the soup, or omit them for a simple, bright soup that's an excellent vehicle for a variety of crunchy and creamy toppings, in addition to being very cooling on hot summer days.

Ingredients

For the broth
3 medium beets, peeled and halved
3 quarts water

To serve
4 hardboiled eggs, chopped
1 cucumber, peeled and chopped
Handful fresh dill, chopped roughly
Green onion, sliced
Sour cream

Process

Place the beets and water in a 4 quart saucepan over high heat. Bring to a boil, then reduce heat and simmer the beets for 30 minutes, or until fork tender. Optionally, you can add a teaspoon of kosher salt for a more savory broth. Allow broth to cool.

Remove the beets and grate them. Add grated beets to broth. Spoon broth into bowls and top with toppings of choice -- we recommend one hardboiled egg per boil, a nice sprinkling of cucumber, green onion, and dill. Finish with a healthy dollop of sour cream.

Beet and Lentil "Burgers"

Makes 15 to 20 patties.

Veggie burgers are a common alternative to their beef sibling in the United States, but I actually came up with this recipe in my little Madrid apartment kitchen one day when I was struck with a very strong craving for one. The original recipe for these patties uses tiny black beluga lentils, which, for their diminutive size, possess a deep, almost smokey flavor that packs a punch. When I make these, I return to my little Madrid apartment and all the amazing moments with friends it held. As an addition on the Rosh Hashanah table, may these not only ensure the removal of your adversaries – as the beet symbolizes – but also allow for the accumulation of friends, old and new, in your new year.

Ingredients

3 tablespoons olive oil
1 cup beluga lentils (or any small, dark lentils will do)
1 onion, finely chopped
2 garlic cloves, minced
1 cup mushrooms (baby bella or white button), sliced
1 green pepper, cored, finely chopped
3 beets, roasted, peeled, and diced small
½ cup canned chopped tomatoes
2 cups water

½ red onion, diced
½ cup breadcrumbs, plus a little more for sprinkling
1 egg
1 ½ tablespoon curry powder
1 ½ teaspoon cumin
1 teaspoon turmeric
1 bay leaf
1 ½ teaspoon salt
½ teaspoon dried oregano

Spicy mayonnaise:

½ cup mayonnaise
2 tablespoons ketchup
1 garlic clove, finely grated
½ teaspoon hot pepper flakes
¼ teaspoon cayenne pepper
½ teaspoon salt
Freshly ground black pepper to taste

Process

To make the burgers: Preheat the oven to 400°F. In a large saucepan, heat the olive oil over medium heat. Once the oil is hot, add the onion and cook until it begins to soften, about 3-5 minutes. Add the garlic, the mushrooms, and the peppers and cook, stirring frequently, until the peppers begin to soften and the mushrooms release their liquid, about 7 minutes.

Add the lentils and the chopped tomatoes, letting cook for one minute to concentrate the tomato flavor. Then, add 1 tablespoon curry powder, 1 teaspoon cumin, the turmeric, the bay leaf, 1 teaspoon of salt, and ground black pepper to taste. Stir the lentils to coat in the spices and cook for 1 minute or so, until the spices release their perfume.

Add the water and bring the lentil mixture to a boil. Lower to a simmer and cook, covered, for 20 minutes, until much of the liquid has been absorbed and the lentils are tender. Once cooked, let cool.

Once lentil mixture is cool, mix in the diced beets, red onion, breadcrumbs, egg, remaining curry powder, oregano, and salt. Mix well until it has the consistency of a thick paste that sticks together when pressed into a patty.

Form the mixture into patties, about 3 inches wide and 1 inch thick. Place on a baking sheet lined with parchment paper. Sprinkle each one with some breadcrumbs.

Bake the patties at 400° for 10 minutes. Then lower the oven temperature to 350°F and bake them for another 30 minutes, flipping once, until they are firm to the touch and the moisture has mostly cooked out.

To make the mayonnaise: Mix all the ingredients together and season with salt and freshly ground black pepper to taste. Serve the burgers with a generous dollop of this sauce.

66 DATE

69	*Middle Eastern Carrot Salad*
71	*Ilana's Date, Apricot, Rice Salad*
72	*Fried Eggplant with Date Syrup*
75	*Alicia's Holiday Chicken with Dried Fruit*
76	*Date Walnut Pie*
79	*Date Pudding Cake*
80	*Date Truffles*

Dates are the only species in the Jewish tradition that are included in both the Seven Species of Israel as well as the Four Species for the celebration of Sukkot. In biblical Israel, the sweet date as well as the date palm from which it comes were essential to life, providing the Israelites both sustenance and shelter. In the rabbinic tradition, those who are considered righteous are often compared to the date palm, which stands tall and straight; in fact in Psalms, it is written that "a *tzadik* [a wise person] blooms like a Date Palm" (Psalms 92:13). This fruit tree possesses further symbolism around the time of Rosh Hashanah because dates are harvested in the late summer and early fall months, just around the time of year that the new year takes place. Given the calendar of their harvest, it seems particularly appropriate that the word for date in Hebrew, *tamar*, should be similar to the word *yitamu*, meaning "to consume" or "to end." When we eat dates on Rosh Hashanah, though, it is to entreat that those who wish to do us harm may be consumed. May their sweetness also temper the end of the old year and help ring in the new.

יְהִי רָצוֹן מִלְּפָנֶיךָ ה' אֱלֹהֵינוּ וֵאלֹהֵי אֲבוֹתֵינוּ וְאִימוֹתֵינוּ, שֶׁיִּתַּמּוּ אוֹיְבֵינוּ וְשׂוֹנְאֵינוּ וְכָל מְבַקְשֵׁי רָעָתֵנוּ

Yehi ratzon milfanecha Adonai eloheinu v'elohei avoteinu v'imoteinu she'yitamu oyveinu v'soneinu v'kol m'vaskshei ra'ateinu.

May it be Your will, God and the God of our ancestors, that there come an end to our enemies, haters and those who wish evil upon us.

Middle Eastern Carrot Salad

Serves 4.

Carrot salads are incredibly common on the Middle Eastern and North African table as accompaniments during meals. This is my version, thin ribbons of carrots tossed with dates, pumpkin seeds, and lightly spiced with cumin and cinnamon. Although a simple and very healthy side dish, the salad's cunning flavor combination of crunchy-tangy-sweet is also quite addictive and large bowls of it have been known to disappear at family gatherings within minutes – so be forewarned.

Ingredients

2 pounds carrots, outer skin removed and peeled in long ribbons with a vegetable peeler
1 cup chopped dates
½ cup pumpkin seeds, toasted
¼ cup olive oil
Juice of 1 lime
½ teaspoon cumin
½ teaspoon cinnamon
1 teaspoon salt
Freshly ground black pepper, to taste

Process

In a large bowl, toss the carrot ribbons, chopped dates, and pumpkin seeds together. Drizzle with the olive oil, lime juice, and season with the spices, salt, and pepper. Toss well to coat the carrot strands. Adjust seasoning as necessary.

Ilana's Date, Apricot, and Rice Salad

Serves 4.

The rice in this recipe acts as a welcome vehicle for whole, juicy apricots sautéed with dates and garlic. Although the combination of apricots, dates, and garlic may seem a little strange, the odorous allium keeps the rice dish from being too sweet. Rice is also a symbol of abundance, which the golden, coin-like shape of the apricots helps to underscore. May this dish help you ring in a prosperous and plentiful new year!

Ingredients

1 ½ cups long grain rice, such as jasmine or basmati
3 cups vegetable broth
½ teaspoon green cardamom seeds
2 tablespoons unsalted butter (optional)
½ cup dates, sliced crosswise in rings
½ cup chopped walnuts
1 cup whole Turkish apricots
1 clove of garlic, thinly sliced crosswise
Juice of half a lemon
6 tablespoons olive oil
1 teaspoon salt

Process

In a large saucepan, place the rice, vegetable broth, ½ teaspoon salt, cardamom seeds, and butter, if using. Bring to a boil and set rice to a simmer for 20 minutes, or until all the liquid is absorbed. Let sit in the pan for 5 minutes, covered. Fluff with a fork and set aside.

Meanwhile, in a large skillet, heat 2 tablespoons olive oil over medium heat. Add the garlic and sauté it for a minute, stirring constantly, until it takes on some color and becomes aromatic. Add the whole apricots and sauté them, about 7 minutes, until they also brown slightly. Add the dates and sauté them until heated through. Take apricot mixture off heat.

Mix cooked apricot mixture with the rice, adding the walnuts. Dress the rice mixture with the olive oil, lemon juice, and remaining salt.

Fried Eggplant with Date Syrup

Serves 5.

Yael contributed this recipe as a twist on a recipe that has roots connecting it to Israel and the Sephardic Jews. Frying eggplant and serving it with honey is very common also to the south of Spain. Indeed, *silan*, a thick syrup made from cooked down dates, is what many believe the "honey" to be in Israel's nickname of "the land of milk and honey." In this dish, the *silan* – readily available in Middle Eastern specialty food stores – offers a complex sweetness as a counterpoint to the savory fried eggplant. The final sprinkle of salt is crucial to bring the dish's flavors in sharp relief.

Ingredients

2 large eggplants, sliced ½" thick with skin still on
1 cup vegetable or olive oil
1 cup flour
1 teaspoon salt

¼ cup date syrup, known as *silan*
Coarse salt, to garnish
Mint leaves, to garnish

Process

Place the flour in a shallow dish or plate. Mix the salt in. Dredge each eggplant slice in flour to lightly coat both sides, shaking off excess.

Meanwhile, heat ¼ of oil in in a large skillet over medium-high heat. Working in batches, fry the eggplant slices, one side at a time, until golden brown and soft, about 2-3 minutes each side. Once each slice is done, remove it to a plate lined with a paper towel to remove excess oil.

Arrange eggplant slices on a plate and sprinkle with salt and mint leaves. Drizzle with date syrup and serve immediately.

Alicia's Holiday Chicken with Dried Fruit

Serves 4-6.

The original recipe for this chicken dish called for pieces of chicken to roast with dried fruit and covered in orange juice and wine, certainly a delicious preparation by one of our community's many talents cooks. In order to increase the "wow" factor of this dish, though, I thought I'd swap in a whole chicken for chicken pieces and stuff it with the fruit-studded mixture instead of topping it. What resulted was a perfectly bronzed, crackly-skinned chicken fit for a celebratory feast – let this chicken be the centerpiece of your Rosh Hashanah meal for a particularly festive main course.

Ingredients

A 7- or 8-pound roasting chicken
1 large sweet onion, cut into small wedges
1 cup dried Turkish apricots
1 cup prunes
1 cup almonds, skins removed
½ cup dates
3 tablespoons olive oil
2 oranges, one juiced and the other cut into slices
1 cup dry white wine
2 teaspoons dried thyme
2 teaspoons salt
1 teaspoon freshly ground black pepper
1 cup chicken broth
8 Celery stalks

Process

Preheat the oven to 425°F. Rinse the chicken and pat dry. Line a roasting pan with the celery stalks. Rub the chicken with orange juice and season all over, including within the cavity, with salt, pepper, and thyme. Drizzle the top with the olive oil.

Mix the apricots, dates, prunes, and almonds in a bowl. Stuff the chicken with the dried fruit mixture, alternating with onion and orange slices. Whatever doesn't fit within the chicken, place in the pan alongside it.

Pour the white wine and chicken broth into the pan and place in the oven. Cook for 10 minutes at 425°F, then lower the oven to 325°F. Roast the chicken, basting occasionally with the cooking liquid, for an hour and half, or until the juices run clear and the chicken's skin is completely golden brown.

Ilva's Date and Walnut Pie

Serves 8

This pie makes for an impressive and sweet finish to any celebratory meal. Unlike a butter-enriched flaky pie crust, the inclusion of egg and baking powder in this recipe ensures both buttery taste and structural stability. The crust allows for the pie's efficient removal from the springform pan it bakes in and, therefore, pan-less presentation to your (hopefully) very impressed guests.

Ingredients

For the dough
1 ¾ cup flour
½ cup (1 stick) unsalted butter, cubed
1 tablespoon of sugar
1 egg plus 1 egg yolk
1 teaspoon baking powder
1 to 3 tablespoons cold water

For the filling
4 eggs, at room temperature
½ cup (1 stick) unsalted butter, at room temperature
1 cup of milk, at room temperature
1/3 cup sugar
2 teaspoons vanilla extract
1 cup chopped dates
½ cup chopped walnuts
Handful whole dates for decorating
Handful whole walnuts for decorating

Process

Make the crust: Preheat the oven to 350°F. In a large bowl, sift the flour with the baking powder. Whisk in the sugar. Using a fork or your hands, mix the butter into the flour mixture, working the butter into the flour until the mixture forms pea-sized lumps. Mix in the egg and egg yolk. Then add the water, one tablespoon at a time, until the mixture forms a coherent dough. Knead the dough to mixture until it stops sticking to your hands and the bowl.

Lightly grease a 10-inch springform pan. Press the dough evenly on the bottom and up the sides of the pan. Refrigerate while preparing the filling.

Make the filling: In a large bowl, cream together the butter and sugar until fluffy. Add the eggs, one at a time, mixing well after each addition. Gradually mix in the milk and vanilla extract. Fold in the chopped dates and walnuts.

Pour the filling into the prepared crust and, if you wish, decorate the top of the pie with the whole dates and walnuts. Bake the pie for 40 minutes, or until the filling sets and the crust is golden brown.

Date Pudding Cake

Serves 8-10.

This sweet, booze-infused cake offers your guests a sweet finish to their meal as well as a reason to prolong the Rosh Hashanah joy. The funny side note to the origin of this recipe, ironically, is that Yael, to whom its credited, found it in a book of recipes from Spanish convents. As many of the monks and nuns of early modern Spain (the early 16th and 17th centuries) were often descended from Jewish families that had voluntarily or been forcibly converted to Catholicism leading up to and during the Inquisition, it seemed appropriate to include it in this book. On a more technical note, make sure to not rush the syrup infusion process, the slower the syrup soaks into the cake, the more evenly the flavor diffuses into it.

Ingredients

For the cake
1 cup chopped dates
1 teaspoon baking soda
1 cup of boiling water
4 tablespoons unsalted butter
1 cup sugar
1 egg
1 cup chopped walnuts
1 ¼ cup flour
1 teaspoon of baking powder
½ teaspoon salt

For the syrup
1 cup water
1 cup sugar
1 teaspoon vanilla
¾ cup rum

Process

Preheat the oven to 350°F. Lightly grease a 10 inch springform pan. In a bowl, stir the dates together with the baking soda and boiling water. Let sit for 10 minutes. Meanwhile, in another large bowl, beat the butter until creamy. Add the sugar and beat, about 5 minutes. Add the egg and beat well to incorporate. Gradually mix in the flour, baking powder, and salt. Stir in the walnuts. To this, add the soaked dates, liquid and all, and mix until well-combined.

Place this mixture in the greased springform and bake for 15 minutes, until a nicely domed sponge has been formed and a toothpick inserted in the center comes out clean. Let cool.

While the cake is baking, mix the water, sugar, vanilla, and rum together until well combined. Brush the syrup over the cake, letting it absorb the liquid between each brushing. Brush with syrup until the cake is completely moistened throughout.

Date Truffles

Makes 18 to 20 truffles.

These truffles are a not-too-sweet dessert for your Rosh Hashanah table. Easy to make, very satisfying, and without any additional sugar, they will be a welcome sweet bite for anyone planning to keep any dietary new year's resolutions. Be forewarned: in keeping with the Rosh Hashanah wish of "being consumed," these truffles disappear quite quickl

Ingredients

8 oz. whole dates
¾ cup hazelnuts or walnuts
½ cup cocoa powder
½ cup shredded coconut (your choice of sweetened or unsweetened)

Process

In a food processor, grind the dates to a smooth paste. Add a tablespoon or two water in case they are too dry. Add the nuts and blend them with the dates until forms a thick paste. Transfer the date-nut mixture to a bowl. Fold the cocoa powd in with a spatula.

Take rounded tablespoonfuls of the mixture and roll into a small ball. Continue un all the date mixture is formed into little balls. Roll each ball in coconut to coat.

Store in the refrigerator until ready to eat.

82 FISH

84 *Orange Salmon*

85 *Forshmak*

87 *Ceutan Fish (Fish with Pipirrana)*

89 *Soy-Silan Salmon*

90 *Yael's Sabbath Cod Fritters*

92 *Guefilte Fish*

Although in this book, we include recipes for fish to be included at your Rosh Hashanah seder, it is actually traditional to include a fish head in the new year seder. This inclusion of just the fish's head is to entreat that we may "be at the head and not the tail" of this year. In other words, the fish head represents the desire for luck and the hopes for a fruitful new year. At the same time, fish – head and body included – have long been a symbolic ingredient in Jewish cooking due to their multiplicity of mystical meanings in the Jewish tradition. From their presence in such important biblical moments as the Flood in Genesis and in Jewish mystical texts, fish are connected to creation, fertility, and prosperity. Indeed, in the Sephardic tradition, fish have even been considered to ward off the Evil Eye. Thus, we hope to entreat all these good wishes with their inclusion in the Rosh Hashanah seder meal.

יְהִי רָצוֹן מִלְפָנֶיךָ ה' אֱלֹהֵינוּ וֵאלֹהֵי אֲבוֹתֵינוּ וְאִמּוֹתֵינוּ, שֶׁ־נִּהְיֶה לְרֹאשׁ וְלֹא לְזָנָב

Yehi ratzon milfanecha Adonai eloheinu v'elohei avoteinu v'imoteinu, she'nihiyeh l'rosh v'lo zanav.

May it be Your will, God and the God of our ancestors, that we be a head and not a tail.

Orange Salmon

Serves 3-4.

Ilana, who contributed this recipe, explains that her two young sons love this dish. The sweetness of the honey counterbalances the acid of the orange juice, making for a simple but satisfying main. The technique of reducing the honey-orange mixture in the oven before the adding the salmon also concentrates its flavor while saving you from dirtying too many pans. This is a great dish should you need a quick-yet-flavorful main dish for your Rosh Hashanah meal. It's also delicious served chilled!

Ingredients

1 pound fillet of salmon
2 oranges
2 tablespoons honey
½ teaspoon salt
Freshly ground black pepper, to taste
Chopped parsley, to garnish

Process

Preheat the oven to 350°F. Juice the two oranges and mix with the honey. Place this mixture on a baking sheet. Cook juice mixture in the oven for 15 minutes, or until it has begun to reduce.

Meanwhile, season the salmon with the salt and pepper. Once the juice mixture has cooked, place the salmon, flesh side down, onto the baking sheet. Bake the salmon for 15 minutes, or until completely cooked through.

Let cool completely before eating or serve warm; garnish with parsley and serve over basmati rice.

Forshmak

Serves up to 4.

Margarita, who comes from Russia, explained that this dish is one that her mother remembers eating for Jewish holidays, prepared by *her* grandmother in the Former Soviet Union. According to Margarita's mom, the herring has to be Russian, but since not everyone can access real Russian herring, for the sake of this book (and the Rosh Hashanah holiday) any good quality oil-packed herring will suffice as a replacement.

Ingredients

5 ounces oil-packed herring fillets
2 eggs, hardbboiled and separated
1 piece of dark or black bread, crust cut of and soaked in water (squeeze out excess water before using)
1 large Granny Smith apple, peeled
3 tablespoon of olive oil
1 tablespoon of vinegar

1/3 of a large onion, chopped and sautéed for 2-3 minutes in 2 tablespoons olive oil
Chopped dill, to garnish

Process

In a food processor, mix the herring fillets, apple, hardboiled egg whites, and bread. Add the oil and vinegar and mix well.

Place mixture in a dish. Crumble the hardboiled egg yolk and top mixture with crumbled yolk and dill to serve.

Ceutan Fish (Fish with Pipirrana)

Serves 4.

This dish comes from the city of origin of Yael, the Reform Community's director. She explains that *the recipe is not inherited from my family but rather was one that mother adopted from a neighbor that became popular in the 70s in Ceuta. The fish, ideally one of a meatier variety that's good for searing, is seared on a griddle for exactly the right amount of time to be later crowned with a salad of fresh vegetables. This salad, which tops the seared fish in order to mix with the cooked fish's juices, is called Pipirrana. It's a nice, fun little name that comes from the south of Andalusia, specifically Cádiz... Cádiz and my North African city of birth, Ceuta, are both port cities, between the European and African continents.* Yael explains that this mix of culinary and cultural influences in the cities on the Strait of Gibraltar contributes to the unique story and delicious history of this salad, which tastes as good atop cod as it does over a meatier fish, such as tuna.

Ingredients

1 pound tuna, Atlantic bonito, tuna, or cod fillet, skinned and de-boned
6 tablespoons olive oil
3 medium salad tomatoes
1 large red pepper
1 sweet onion
¾ cup finely chopped parsley
1 cucumber (optional)

1 teaspoon salt
½ teaspoon freshly ground black pepper

Juice of 1 lemon

Process

Finely chop the tomatoes, red pepper, onion, and cucumber (if using). Mix to combine in a bowl. Add the parsley, lemon juice, 3 tablespoons of olive oil, ½ teaspoon of salt, and a generous pinch of pepper. Mix well to combine and let rest while cooking the fish.

Meanwhile, heat the remaining 3 tablespoons of oil in a large, shallow skillet over medium-high heat. Once the oil is heated, place the fish in the pan. Cook for 3 minutes on one side, then flip to other side and cook for 3 more minutes, until just cooked through. Remove from heat and top with the Pipirrana.

Soy-Silan Salmon

Serves 4.

Alicia explains that the inspiration for this dish comes from her time living in Israel. While there, she discovered that *silan*, the thick date syrup, was a delicious substitute for honey. Now back in Spain, she continues to use silan in most dishes that call for honey, including this salmon, which lends them a sweet complexity. The combination of soy sauce and *silan* in this recipe's marinade helps to elevate the baked salmon from a common fish to the star of your Rosh Hashanah meal.

Ingredients

1 lb salmon fillet
3 tablespoons silan (date honey)
5 tablespoons soy sauce
Juice of 1 lemon
½ teaspoon freshly ground black pepper
2 tablespoons olive oil
1 tablespoon water

Process

Mix the *silan*, soy sauce, lemon juice, black pepper, olive oil, and oil together. Pour over salmon fillet and let marinate in the refrigerator for 2 hours.

Preheat the oven to 375°F. Place the salmon fillet on a baking sheet and pour marinade over top of the salmon. Cook for 15 minutes, or until the salmon is cooked through but not dry and the marinade has reduced.

Remove the salmon from the baking dish and reserve reduced marinade. Serve pieces of fish drizzled with the marinade with extra lemon wedges.

Yael's Sabbath Cod Fritters

Makes about 20 fritters.

This recipe comes from the mother of the president of the Comunidad, Yael, who originally comes from Ceuta, one of the two Spanish territories in the north of Africa. Although I will note here that salted cod is a particularly Spanish ingredient, its usage going back to medieval times, I want to let Yael's words about this recipe introduce it: *this is a recipe that my mother always made and has always loved, but recently she told me that my grandmother in Morocco made it, too. However, it's not a Jewish recipe per se. I suppose it arrived there through Andalusian – that is to say, southern Spanish – and Spanish influence in Morocco. In fact, it's very popular in the south of Spain. It's a complete homage to how recipes and flavors cross seas (in this case, a strait – that of Gibraltar) back and forth, various times and how Jews absorb culinary traditions from the world around us and vice versa.*

Ingredients

14 oz. salt cod, de-salted (see process below) and shredded
1 cup finely chopped parsley
4 cloves of garlic, minced
1 ½ cups flour
1 cup water
¾ cup olive oil

Process

To de-salt the cod, place it in a large bowl and fill the bowl to the top with cold water. Let sit for an hour. After an hour, replace the water with fresh cold water and let sit another 2 hours. Do this again for at least a total of 8 hours, up to 24 hours (you can let it soak in the fridge overnight.

Once the cod has been de-salted, shred it with a fork. Mix the cod with the garlic, parsley, and 1 cup of water. Then, a spoonful at a time, gradually add the flour until the mixture reaches the consistency of a slightly water-y dough.

Meanwhile, heat the olive in a skillet over medium-high heat. Once the oil is hot, drop rounded tablespoonfuls of the cod mixture into the pan. Fry on the first side until golden, about 3-5 minutes and flip, frying the other side, about another 3 minutes. Remove the cod fritters the a plate lined with a paper towel to remove excess oil.

 Serve with sour cream, apple sauce, or with a lemon wedge and more chopped parsley.

Guefilte Fish

Makes about 24 gefilte fish patties/balls.

A book about Jewish food would be remiss if it didn't mention gefilte fish, that polarizing fish dish that breeds such intense feelings of love and hate. Indeed, when we asked for recipes we received many, including one from a community member's Polish grandmother in Buenos Aires. Unfortunately we could only use one. That being said, I thought it important to note that this recipe is one that is particular to the Comunidad, not only for some of the culinary idiosyncrasies of the recipe – including the tomato marmalade, briefly sautéed onion, and use of olive oil – but also because of its unique place on the Reform Jewish Community of Madrid's celebratory table in addition to, on occasion, our weekly Sabbath meals. It is for that reason that we maintained the hispanized spelling of gefilte – *guefilte* – for this recipe: because it holds a special place for our Spanish community and, therefore hopefully, on your holiday table as well.

Ingredients

1 pound trout fillets, skin and bones removed
1 pound perch fillets, skin and bones removed
1 pound filleted hake, skin and bones removed
1 onion, chopped and sautéed for 2-3 minutes in 2 tablespoons of olive oil
1 raw onion, cut into eighths
3 eggs
1 teaspoon salt

½ teaspoon freshly ground pepper
½ cup water
4 tablespoons sugar (optional)

For the broth:
1 fish head
1 onion, cut into eighths
4 carrots, peeled and sliced in 1" thick rounds
4 cups water
1 teaspoon salt
1 teaspoon pepper corns (optional)
3 tablespoons sugar (optional)

To serve:

Tomato marmalade
Horseradish

92

Process

Preheat the oven to 350°F. Using a food processor fitted with a blade attachment, finely grind the fish in batches. (If you like, you can also ask the fishmonger to do this for you.) Place in a bowl and mix until the three fish are well-combined.

Then, in the food processor, finely chop the onion cooked in oil and raw onion. With the food processor running, add the salt, pepper, sugar (if using), eggs, and water and pulse to combine. Reserve in another bowl.

Alternating between the ground fish and onion-egg mixture, add small quantities of each to the food processor, pulsing for 30 seconds between to combine all the ingredients well. Pour mixture into a bowl and stir once or twice with a wooden spoon, to ensure all ingredients are well-mixed.

Lay the fish head, carrots, and onions in a large roasting pan with a depth of at least 3 inches and at least 13 inches by 9 inches in dimension. Take rounded tablespoonfuls of the fish mixture, shaping them into balls or patties. Place them on top of the onions and carrots. Gently pour the water in the side of the pan to fill it, until it just covers the gefilte fish balls. Sprinkle the mixture with the salt and peppercorns and sugar (if using).

Place in oven and cook, uncovered, for 30 to 40 minutes, or until the gefilte fish balls are firm, the vegetables are fork tender, and the cooking liquid is gelatinous. Reserve the cooked carrots and onions to serve.

To serve, place one to two gefilte fish balls on a plate with some of the reserved carrots and onions, topped with tomato marmalade and horseradish.

94 HONEY

96 *Alicia's Challah*

98 *Honeyed Turnips*

99 *Honey Chicken*

101 *Turkish Poppy Seed Cake*

102 *Yael's Honey Cigars*

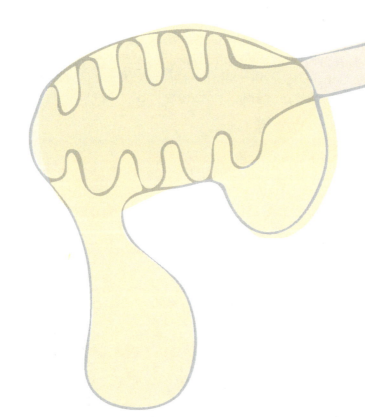

In the Jewish tradition, honey is one of the defining features of the land of Israel, "the land of milk and honey." During biblical times, the word for honey in Hebrew, *devash*, actually connoted both honey made from bees as well as honey made from boiled-down fruits, like dates. Beyond its connection to Israel, though, honey possesses deep symbolism within Judaism due to its uniquely sweet and healing properties. Indeed, in the Talmud, the rabbinic sages wrote that honey can "restore the sight of the eyes" (Babylonian Talmud, Yoma 83b:7). Indeed, this healing aspect of the sweet liquid may be why honey is included in the blessing for renewal in the new year. May the sweetness it adds to your Rosh Hashanah table restore and renew you in the new year.

יְהִי רָצוֹן מִלְּפָנֶיךָ ה' אֱלֹהֵינוּ וֵאלֹהֵי אֲבוֹתֵינוּ, שֶׁתְּחַדֵּשׁ עָלֵינוּ שָׁנָה טוֹבָה וּמְתוּקָה כַּדְּבַשׁ

Yehi ratzon milfanecha Adonai eloheinu v'elohei avoteinu v'imoteinu, she't'chadesh aleinu shanah tovah u'metukah ka'devash.

May it be Your will, God and the God of our ancestors, that You renew for us a year good and sweet like honey.

Alicia's Challah

1 circular loaf or 2 braded loafs.

Challah is an indispensable part of the weekly Sabbath table. On Rosh Hashanah, however, the special circular loaves baked for the holiday take on an even more special significance as symbols of the continuity between years. Alicia's recipe is particularly apt for this holiday and this cookbook, as it utilizes honey to sweeten the enriched dough and infuse the loaves with even more positive symbolism for the year ahead. Feel free to knead some raisins or other dried fruit into the dough to add just that extra bit of holiday sweetness.

Ingredients

½ cup olive oil
½ cup honey
1 tablespoon salt
3 eggs
2 cups of lukewarm water
2 ounces fresh yeast

8 cups of flour, plus 1 more cup for kneading
1 egg, beaten, mixed with 1 tablespoon water
Sesame seeds (optional)

Process

Preheat the oven to 350°F. In a large bowl, mix together the olive oil and honey. Then, add the rest of the ingredients in the given order and mix until the dough starts to come together.

Turn the dough out onto a floured surface and knead for 10 minutes, or until it forms a smooth ball with an elastic surface. Place the ball of dough in a different bowl that has been greased lightly with oil. Cover the bowl with a towel and let the dough rise for an hour, or until it has doubled in size.

Once doubled, remove the dough from the bowl and knead again for 5 minutes. Place it back in the bowl and let the dough rise for another hour.

Once it has risen again, remove the dough from the bowl and form a braid. Below we give two options for braiding, one a traditional 3-part braid and the other a circular challah special for Rosh Hashanah.

To form a three-part braid: This recipe forms 2 3-part braid loaves. Split the ball of dough in half, and then split those halves into even thirds. Starting with one group of three pieces of dough, roll the pieces into 3 strips of even length. Then, braid the pieces together to form a loaf. Repeat this process with the other half of the dough.

To form a circular challah: This recipe will make 1 large circular challah loaf. Divide the dough into 4 even pieces. Arrange two strips parallel to each other, then lay the other two strips perpendicular to the first two, overlapping alternate strands to form a hashtag shape where they meet in the middle. Take the strands under the center and place them over the strands to their right. Then, take the strands that the first strands went over, and pull them over the strands to their left. Repeat this process until all the length of the dough strands has been used up. Tuck any odd bumps or extra dough underneath to form a round.

Place the loaf (or loaves) on a baking sheet and brush with the egg-water mixture. Sprinkle with sesame seeds, if using. Place in oven and bake 30-40 minutes, or until golden brown and hollow sounding when tapped on the bottom. Let cool on a rack.

Honeyed Turnips

Serves 4.

Although it's quite common to find honey combined with fruit, this recipe struck me for the combination of turnips with the sweet golden liquid. Turnips aren't necessarily the most popular of root vegetables, but boiled until tender and graced with honey and walnuts, they turn into a magical side dish, perfect to accompany meat-centered main dishes. Give this dish a try if you're looking to augur in sweetness in unusual places in your new year.

Ingredients

2 pounds turnips, peeled and grated
1 cup sugar
1 cup honey
1 cup water
1 ½ cup chopped walnuts
Pinch of salt

Process

In a large pot, place the grated turnip and cover with water. Bring to a boil over high heat and boil the grated turnip until tender, about 7-10 minutes. Drain the turnip and rinse with cold water.

Meanwhile, in a large skillet with a tight-fitting lid, mix the sugar, water, and honey. Bring mixture to a boil and add the turnip. Once you add the turnip, immediately turn the heat to low. Simmer the turnip mixture, covered, until all the liquid is absorbed.

Uncover the pan and stir in the walnuts. Let the turnip cook for another 5 minutes, or until golden brown. Serve warm.

Honey Chicken

Serves 6-8.

Adapted from a recipe from Joan Nathan's *Jewish Holiday Cookbook*, my mom has prepared this delicious chicken dish for my family's Rosh Hashanah meal since before I can remember. To me, this dish is what the new year tastes like: breaded chicken drenched in an addictive orange-ginger-honey sauce – a sauce that could easily be drunk straight from the pan. The scent of this chicken cooking is how I know the new year is coming. In my house, we make this dish the day before we plan to serve it; it's much better the next day, when the flavors have had a chance to meld. It's divine served over basmati rice, which creates an excellent, much more elegant way of sopping up as much of the delectable sauce as possible.

Ingredients

- 2 eggs
- 2 teaspoons water
- 1 cup breadcrumbs
- 1 teaspoon salt
- ¼ teaspoon pepper
- 2 3-pound fryers (I use 6 pounds of mixed chicken pieces: thighs, drumsticks, and wings with skin on are particularly important for the flavor of the dish)
- ½ cup vegetable or olive oil
- 1 cup hot water (should be hot enough to dissolve the honey, but it doesn't need to be boiling)
- ¼ cup honey
- 1 cup orange juice (store bought is fine)
- 2 tablespoons grated fresh ginger

Process

Beat the eggs with the 2 teaspoons of water. In another bowl, mix the breadcrumbs with the salt and pepper. Dip the chicken in the egg mixture to coat and then the breadcrumbs, making sure to distribute the crumbs in an even coating all over the piece of chicken.

Heat the oil in a heavy skillet (very important: DO NOT put the chicken in a skillet that's not hot enough; it will just absorb grease and won't taste as good) and brown the chicken on all sides. Preheat the oven to 325°F/165°C. Place the chicken in an oven-proof casserole with a lid or a roasting pan that you can cover with aluminum foil.

In another bowl, combine the orange juice, honey, and hot water. Pour the mixture over the chicken and sprinkle the grated ginger on top. Cover the chicken and simmer it in the oven for 45 minutes (sometimes I even let it go for an hour), basting occasionally. If serving the next day: Store the dish, covered, in the refrigerator. Reheat it at 350°F/175°C for about 15-20 minutes, until warmed through.

Ilva's Turkish Poppy Seed Cake

Serves 8-10.

For the amount of sugar and honey in the syrup that drenches this cake, it somehow manages to not be overly sweet. Garnished with whipped cream, this cake makes for a delightful finish to a Rosh Hashanah dinner or, topped with a generous dollop of plain Greek yogurt, a very sweet breakfast for your new year's day.

Ingredients

For the cake
1 cup flour
1 cup semolina
1 cup poppy seeds
1 cup sugar
1 tablespoon baking powder
½ teaspoon salt
1 cup olive oil
1 cup milk
3 eggs
1 teaspoon vanilla extract

For the syrup
10 tablespoons honey
3 cups water
1 ½ cup sugar
Juice of 1 lemon

Process

Preheat the oven to 350°F. Grease a 13" by 9" baking pan, line it with parchment paper, then grease and flour the paper-lined pan.

Make the cake: Mix the flour, semolina, sugar, baking powder, and salt in a large bowl. In another bowl, whisk together the olive oil, milk, eggs, and vanilla extract until well-combined. Pour the wet mixture with the dry mixture and mix well. Add the poppy seeds. Pour the mixture into the pan and bake 40 – 45 minutes, or until a toothpick comes out the center clean.

Make the syrup: While the cake is baking, combine all syrup ingredients in a saucepan and bring to a boil. Boil the mixture for 15 minutes, until it becomes sticky in consistency and reduces by a quarter. Once the cake is out of the oven, let it cool for 5 minutes. Then, with a toothpick, poke the cake all over. Pour the syrup onto the cake gradually so that it absorbs it evenly. Serve cake with a generous dollop of plain Greek yogurt.

Yael's Honey Cigars

Makes about 30 cigars.

As Yael explains of this recipe, *the honey cigars are an central part of every holiday. It's a must for b'nai mitzvah, brit mila, and, of course, Rosh Hashanah – for that bath of aromatic honey. My mother never made them, even though they were very popular in Morocco,* near Ceuta, where Yael is from. Her mother *preferred to order them to be eaten at home.* However, as Yael explains, *the history of the cigar is triangular in the very same form as the way this cookie is prepared, because I learned this Sephardic pastry technique from a Muslim woman who worked for a Jewish family from my city. The fact is, this dessert is also typical of Moroccan pastry, although there it appears in the form of a triangle, not a cigar, and is called* briouate. Not only does this recipe symbolize the three-sided connection between our history and that of others, but it also represents as a delicious, honey-soaked invitation for sweetness in the new year.

Ingredients

2 ¼ cup fine almond flour
2 tablespoons confectioner's sugar
2 teaspoons ground cinnamon
¼ teaspoon ground cloves
½ teaspoon ground cardamom
Dash of nutmeg

Pinch of salt
4 tablespoons orange blossom water
Package of wonton wrappers or brik leaves
½ cup (1 stick) butter, melted
1 egg, beaten
1 ½ cups honey

Process

Preheat the oven to 350°F. In a large bowl, whisk together the almond flour, confectioner's sugar, spices, and salt. Add 3 tablespoons of the orange blossom water (or just water, if you don't have orange blossom water). Take teaspoon sized pieces of the mixture and form small balls. Set aside on a plate.

Take the wonton wrappers (or brik leaves) and cut a curved edge between two opposite corners to form a fan shape. Take a ball of the almond mixture and roll it slightly to form a small log. Place the filling at the bottom of the curved edge of the wrapper. Fold the wrapper over the filling once, evenly pushing the filling out lengthwise. Fold in the left and right corners of the wrapper, on either side of the filling, then continue to roll the wrapper up tightly towards the remaining corner to form a thin cigar shape. Before completely rolling the cigar, brush the top corner with a little bit of melted butter so as to seal the cigar completely. Proceed until all wrappers and balls of filling are used.

Place the cigars on a baking sheet and brush them with the beaten egg. Bake them, turning once, for 12 to 15 minutes or until they are golden all over. Meanwhile, heat up the honey and the remaining tablespoon of orange blossom water in a saucepan over medium heat. Once the cigars are out of the oven, while they are still warm, pour the heated honey over them and let them rest until cool.

104 LEEK

106   *Noa's Leek Salad*

107   *Adele's Leek Crema*

109   *Roasted Leeks with Balsamic Reduction & Goat Cheese*

110   *Borekas de Prasa*

112   *Leek Kofte*

114   *Pasta with Leek Sauce and Salmon*

Leeks have long had a place of importance for the Jewish people. Across many Jewish cultural groups, leeks are a central and beloved ingredient of the Jewish culinary repertoire. In fact, this oblong allium was one of the food that the ancient Israelites missed during their forty-year wanderings in the dessert: in Numbers 11:5 the Israelite's invoke divine anger when they complain "we remember the fish which we ate in Egypt freely; the cucumbers, watermelons, leeks, onions, and garlic." Needless to say, leeks have been present in the Jewish culinary tradition for quite a long time and, although they are a common ingredient across Jewish culinary repertoires, they take on a special valence for the Rosh Hashanah seder. The Aramaic root for the word "leek" is *karti*, which is similar to the Hebrew word *yikartu*, which means to "cut off." Thus, when we say the yehi ratzon over the leek on Rosh Hashanah, we wish that our enemies may be cut off in the upcoming year – but never our supply of leeks!

יְהִי רָצוֹן מִלְּפָנֶיךָ ה' אֱלהֵינוּ וֵאלֹהֵי אֲבוֹתֵינוּ וְאִימוֹתֵינוּ, שֶׁיִּכָּרְתוּ אוֹיְבֵינוּ וְשׂוֹנְאֵינוּ וְכָל מְבַקְשֵׁי רָעָתֵנוּ

Yehi ratzon milfanecha Adonai eloheinu v'elohei avoteinu v'imoteinu, she'yikartu oyveinu v'soneinu v'kol m'vakshei ra'ateinu.

May it be Your will, God and the God of our ancestors, that our enemies, haters, and those who wish evil upon us shall be cut down.

Noa's Leek Salad

Serves 4.

It's unusual to eat leeks raw, but in this salad, they are sliced so thin they offer a crunchy and welcoming canvas for lemon juice, olive oil, and salt play on. With the addition of the green peppers, this salad offers a lovely alternative to lettuce based side dishes on your Rosh Hashanah table. Indeed, this unusual salad is a regular addition to Noa's Sabbath table. Be sure to pick leeks at their freshest and most tender, and wash them well to remove any grit.

Ingredients

2 lbs leeks, white and light green parts only
2 Italian green peppers
1 teaspoon salt
6 tablespoons olive oil
Juice of 1 lemon

Process

Place the leeks in a big bowl and cover with cold water. Sprinkle with a tablespoon of salt and let sit for half an hour. Drain the leeks, rinsing well with more cold water, and let dry. Slice leeks in paper thin rounds. Slice the green peppers in paper thin strips, cutting them to about an inch in length. Mix the peppers and leeks together in a large bowl.

Salt the leek and pepper mixture, then add the olive oil and lemon juice. Toss thoroughly to coat everything.

Adele's Leek Crema

Serves 6-8.

This recipe comes from a community member who is a member of both the Reform Jewish Community of Madrid and of our sister community in Barcelona, the Bet Shalom Progressive Jewish Community. She inherited this recipe from her aunt Regina, whose familiar roots incidentally go back to Jewish family who left Barcelona centuries ago to settle in Italy. In a happy twist of fate, Adele now lives in Barcelona and her recipes are famous in both the Madrid Comunidad and the Bet Shalom community – especially her Italian challah, a brioche-like oaf over which she drizzles a sugar syrup. Adele's aunt Regina always prepared this Leek Crema and the Pasta with Leek Sauce and Salmon (page 114) for family celebrations in the fall and winter, as she associated the warmth and comfort of these dishes with the Rosh Hashanah season. Should you have any of this soup leftover, you can use it to prepare the aforementioned Pasta with Leek Sauce and Salmon instead of making the leek cream sauce all over again.

Ingredients

- 2 medium onions, cut into large chunks
- 2 large leeks, dark green parts and roots cut off, white and light green parts cut in large chunks
- 2 medium waxy potatoes, peeled and cut into large chunks
- 8 cups water
- 1 teaspoon salt
- ½ teaspoon freshly ground black pepper
- 1 ½ tablespoons olive oil
- 7 tablespoons unsalted butter
- ½ cup grated Parmesan, plus more for garnish
- One ¾ oz wedge Laughing Cow cheese (optional)
- Croutons, for serving (optional)
- Olive oil, for garnish (optional)

Process

Place the onions, leeks, potatoes, salt, pepper, and 1 ½ tablespoons olive oil in a large pot. Cover with the 8 cups of water. Set the vegetables and water over high heat and bring to a boil. Once the mixture boils, lower the heat to a simmer and let cook, covered, for one hour. After an hour, once all the vegetables are cooked, take the pot off the heat. Add the butter and let the mixture sit for 5 minutes, so that the butter melts. Then, add the parmesan cheese. Using an immersion blender or a blender, process the water, vegetable, and cheese mixture until it forms a smooth, creamy soup. At this point, if you're using the Laughing Cow wedge, you can blend it into the mixture.

To serve, ladle the soup into a bowl and top with breadcrumbs, parmesan shavings, and a drizzle of olive oil.

Roasted Leeks with Balsamic Reduction & Goat Cheese

Serves 4.

Leeks are not often the star of the show at the dinner table. This lack of leek usage, though, is a real shame – when permitted to shine, leeks reveal a surprising level of complexity in their flavor. Roasting them mellows out the more intense onion-y flavors, offering a canvas upon which the sweet acidity of the balsamic reduction and tangy creaminess of the goat cheese create a beautiful vignette. What better time than at your new year's meal to give new ingredients their moment in the spotlight, especially one that symbolizes freedom in the new year.

Ingredients

1 lb leeks, cleaned, green parts removed, white and light green parts sliced in 2 inch pieces
4 oz goat cheese
½ cup balsamic vinegar
1 tablespoon sugar
3 tablespoons olive oil
½ teaspoon dried thyme
½ teaspoon salt
Freshly ground pepper

Process

Preheat oven to 375°F. Place leeks on a baking sheet and drizzle with olive oil. Sprinkle with salt, pepper, and thyme and stir briefly to evenly coat. Place in the oven and roast for 30 to 35 minutes, or until the leeks brown around the edges and soften.

Meanwhile, place the balsamic vinegar and sugar in a saucepan over medium heat. Bring to a boil and continue to simmer the mixture, stirring frequently, until it reduces by half.

Once leeks have come out of the oven, dot with goat cheese and drizzle with the balsamic reduction.

Borekas de Prasa

Makes about 25 borekas.

Adapted from two of the foremost works on Jewish cooking, Claudia Roden's *The Book of Jewish Food* and Gil Marks' *Olive Trees and Honey: A Treasury of Vegetarian Recipes from Jewish Communities Around the World*, these borekas are a classic Sephardic recipe. In the Sephardic tradition, it is not a holiday or a well-observed Sabbath unless there are borekas present. These delicious half-moon pastries adorn both weekly Sabbath tables and holiday spreads alike, so we would be remiss if we did not include a recipe for them in this book – to both honor the Sephardic tradition and to highlight how delicious these leek-filled pastries are. Add these delightful hand pies to your celebratory menu and you'll soon crave them in your everyday.

For the dough (masa):
½ cup vegetable oil (sunflower oil also works)
8 tablespoons unsalted butter
½ cup water
½ teaspoon salt
About 3 cups flour
1 egg for brushing the tops of the borekas
Sesame seeds for sprinkling on the borekas

For the filling (gomo de prasa):
3 tablespoons unsalted butter or olive oil
12 ounces leeks (white and light green parts only), washed and chepped (about 3 cups)
1 onion, chopped
¼ cup water
3 large eggs, lightly beaten
¾ cup matza meal or fresh bread crumbs
1 teaspoon kosher salt
Ground black pepper

Process

Preheat the oven to 350°F. Grease two 9"x13" baking sheets.

Make the dough: Heat the oil and butter in a pan over low heat until the butter melts. Take the mixture off the heat and let cool a few minutes. Add the water and salt and beat well.

Transfer the butter mixture to a bowl and add the flour to it gradually. Add enough flour to make a soft, greasy dough that holds together in a ball. Begin mixing in the flour with a fork and then work it in with your hands when the dough begins to come together. You don't want to handle the dough too much; as soon as it holds together stop mixing. Cover the dough in a plastic wrap and let it rest at room temperature for 20 minutes. Don't put the dough in the refrigerator because this will make it too hard to work with. It should have the same texture as an ear lobe.

Make the filling: In a large skillet, melt the butter over medium heat. Add the leeks and onion and sauté until slightly softened, about 5 minutes. Add the water, cover, and cook until the leeks are tender, another 5-7 minutes. Uncover and cook, stirring frequently, until the liquid evaporates. Let cool, then stir in the remaining ingredients.

Make the borekas: Take walnut-sized lumps and roll each into a little ball. Press and squash the ball between your palms until it's a flat circle. Put the flat circle on your counter and using your palm stretch and flatten into a 4-inch round.

Put a heaping teaspoon of filling in the middle of each round. Be careful not to over-stuff your borekas – they'll explode in the oven. Fold the dough over the filling into a half-moon shape. Pinch the edges firmly together to seal the borekas. It is traditional to pinch, fold and twist the dough around the edges of the borekas once they have been sealed.

Place the borekas on an oiled tray and brush them with the egg that has been mixed with a bit of water. Sprinkle with sesame seeds if you like.

Bake the borekas for about 30 minutes or until they are golden. Serve immediately. They can be stored and reheated, or do very well frozen and reheated in a 350°F oven for about 20 minutes.

Leek Kofte

Makes about 30 patties.

This recipe comes from a community member, Rudi, who hails from Turkey, where this recipe is quite common and goes by many names. This is his mother's recipe. Indeed, whether they are called *kofte* or *kufta* – the two other common names for these meatballs – they are found all over the Middle Eastern, Mediterranean, and North African regions. And it's no wonder – these leek meatballs make a particularly auspicious and delicious centerpiece or hors d'oeuvre for your Rosh Hashanah meal.

Ingredients

1 pound leeks, cleaned and thinly sliced to the light green part (about 2 cups thinly sliced leeks)
3 tablespoons olive oil
½ pound ground beef (20% fat preferable)
2 medium waxy potatoes, such as Yukon Gold, peeled and cubed
1 cup flour
2 eggs, lightly beaten

1 cup vegetable or olive oil, for frying
2 tsp salt
½ tsp. freshly ground black pepper
½ tsp. Aleppo pepper or smoked paprika (optional)
Chopped parsley, to garnish
Lemon wedges, to garnish

Process

Set the potatoes in a 4 quart saucepan with 1 teaspoon of salt and fill the pan with enough water to cover the potatoes. Boil the potatoes for 10 minutes, or until fork tender. Reserving ½ cup of the cooking water, drain the potatoes and mash them thoroughly with a fork or masher, so no chunks remain.

Meanwhile, heat the 3 tablespoons olive oil in a large skillet over medium heat. Add the leeks and sauté for 5 minutes, until the leeks soften. Pour the ½ cup reserved cooking water over the leeks and cook, stirring occasionally, for another 10 minutes, until the leeks are completely soft. Let cool for 10 minutes, or until the leeks can be handled. Over a bowl or the sink, squeeze the leeks to express the excess liquid and place them in a separate bowl.

After extracting the excess liquid from the leeks, combine them with the ground beef, mashed potatoes, ¼ cup of flour, eggs, 1 teaspoon salt, black pepper, and Aleppo pepper or paprika if using. Mix thoroughly. The mixture should have the consistency of a thick paste.

Heat ½ cup of oil in a large skillet over medium-high heat. Meanwhile, place the remaining flour in a shallow dish. Working in batches, take walnut-sized pieces of the leek-meat mixture and form small meatballs. Roll the balls in flour so that they are lightly coated in it, and place in the hot pan. Fry the meatballs, slightly flattening them with the spatula to form small patties, cooking them on one side for 5 minutes, then flipping and cooking for another 3 minutes. They should be fried until browned and cooked through all the way. Halfway through the frying process, replace the oil with the remaining ½ cup.

Once the patties are fully cooked, remove them from the pan and place them on a plate lined with paper towel to remove the excess oil. Serve garnished with chopped parsley and a lemon wedge.

Pasta with Leek Sauce and Salmon

Serves 4.

This is another recipe for leeks from Adele, one of our community members with Italian heritage. In case you've made Adele's Leek Crema (page 107) and have a little extra leftover, you can actually use the soup and save yourself some steps in preparing the leek cream of this recipe from scratch. Be sure to only cook your pasta to *al dente*; it'll continue cooking in the pan once you add the leek cream sauce and the salmon. This makes a wonderful pescetarian/vegetarian-friendly main for your Rosh Hashanah meal and is incredibly comforting for when Rosh Hashanah falls on the autumn side of the holiday season.

Ingredients

1 lb salmon fillet, skin and bones removed
1 pound farfalle or parpadelle pasta
1 medium onion, thinly sliced
½ pound leeks, dark green parts and roots removed, cut into ½ inch pieces
4 cups water
2 tablespoons unsalted butter
Juice of 1 orange

Zest of 1 orange
3 tablespoons of olive oil plus 1 more tablespoon
3 teaspoon salt
½ teaspoon freshly ground black pepper
½ cup grated parmesan (optional)

Process

In a saucepan, heat 3 tablespoons of olive oil over medium. Add the sliced onion and cook until they start to soften, about 3 minutes. Add the pieces of leek and stir well to combine with the onion. Continue to sauté the leeks and onions, stirring frequently, until they start to brown, about 8 to 10 minutes. Then, add the water, ½ teaspoon salt, and pepper to the leek and onion mixture. Bring to a boil over high heat, then lower the flame to medium and continue to cook the mixture at a vigorous simmer for 30 minutes.

Meanwhile, heat the other tablespoon of olive oil in a skillet over medium-high. While the oil is heating, sprinkle the salmon with ½ teaspoon of salt. Once the oil is hot, add the salmon and sear the one side for 3 minutes, then flip the salmon and sear the other side, another 3 minutes. Once the salmon starts to form a golden crust, add the orange juice. Bring down the heat to low, and simmer the salmon until it's cooked through, about 10 minutes. Once the salmon is done, remove the pan from the heat. Take the salmon from the pan and place it on a cutting board. Then, using a fork, delicately shred the salmon in ½ inch to 1 inch chunks. If there's any sauce left in the pan that the salmon cooked in, mix the salmon into it. Reserve.

Set a large pot of water to boil with 2 teaspoons of water. Once the water boils, put the pasta in and cook until it is cooked through but al dente, about 8-10 minutes. Drain the pasta, reserving ½ cup of the cooking water.

While the pasta boils, remove the leek-onion mixture from the heat and add the 2 tablespoons of butter. Using an immersion or a regular blender, blend the mixture until it is smooth and creamy in consistency.

In another sauté pan, mix together the pasta, leek-onion cream, and the salmon. If the mixture seems a little dry, pour in some of the reserved pasta cooking liquid to help fully coat the pasta. Mix in the parmesan if using. Serve with extra parmesan grated on top.

116 POMEGRANATE

119 *Festive Pomegranate Salad*

120 *Pomegranate Gazpacho*

123 *Quinoa Salad with Pomegranate, Orange & Watercress*

125 *Marisa's Jewelled Rice*

126 *The Israeli Ambassador's Cauliflower*

129 *Pomegranate Steak*

Pomegranates are well-known for their large number of seeds – 365, as many as the days of the year. They occupy a particularly significant symbolic place in the Jewish tradition, too; in fact, they are one of the seven species in Deuteronomy used to describe the land of Israel, "a land of wheat and barley, of vines, figs, and pomegranates, a land of olive trees and honey" (Deuteronomy 8:8). In the Talmud, too, the Jewish people are identified with the pomegranate and its abundance of seeds; in many places in the Talmud, the rabbis, such as Reish Lakish, say that even those least worthy in the Jewish community are as full of good deeds – *mitzvot* – as "a pomegranate is full of seeds" (Babylonian Talmud, Chagigah 27a). In that way, when we eat pomegranates at our new year seder, we entreat that our merits may multiply and that we also be filled with *mitzvot*, just like this beautiful seed-filled fruit.

יְהִי רָצוֹן מִלְפָנֶיךָ ה' אֱלֹהֵינוּ וֵאלֹהֵי אֲבוֹתֵינוּ וְאִמוֹתֵינוּ,
שֶׁנִּהְיֶה מְלֵאִים מִצְוֹת כָּרִמּוֹן

*Yehi ratzon milfanecha Adonai eloheinu v'elohei avoteinu v'imoteinu,
she'nihiyeh m'lei'im mitzvot ka'rimon.*

May it be Your will, God and the God of our ancestors, that we be filled with mitzvot like the pomegranate's seeds.

Festive Pomegranate Salad

Serves 8-10.

There is nothing that symbolizes abundance as well as a big, beautiful, fresh salad chock full of fruit and nuts. This is exactly the salad for a big celebratory occasion: bright, vibrant, and filled to the brim with juicy kumquats and pomegranate seeds. When you serve this salad, your guests will be able to rejoice bountiful food and ring in an abundance of blessings for the new year.

Ingredients

- 1 bunch of escarole lettuce
- 2 pomegranates, seeded
- 1 pint kumquats, halved
- ½ cup walnuts, roughly chopped
- 1 medium shallot, thinly sliced
- 4 oz goat cheese, crumbled
- ¼ cup olive oil
- 3 tablespoons pomegranate juice
- 2 tablespoons balsamic vinegar
- ½ teaspoon salt
- Freshly ground pepper
- ½ teaspoon tarragon
- 1 teaspoon cumin seeds

Process

Wash and roughly tear the escarole; place in a bowl. Add pomegranate seeds, kumquats, walnuts, shallots, goat cheese, and cumin seeds. Toss.

In another bowl, mix the balsamic vinegar and pomegranate juice together. Add salt, pepper, and tarragon. Then, gradually whisk in the balsamic vinegar to make an emulsion.

Pour the dressing over the salad and toss well, until all leaves are coated.

Pomegranate Gazpacho

Serves 8-10.

Of all the many Iberian foods, none are so recognizably Spanish as gazpacho, that garlicky tomato elixir so essential to counteract the long hot days of the Spanish summer. Here we've taken the recipe and given it a Rosh Hashanah-appropriate twist using pomegranate juice as the liquid canvas for fresh summer bounty, including cucumbers, peppers, and red onion. The tart sweetness of the juice offers a novel and refreshing way to enjoy this delicious cold soup, a perfect starter or accompaniment to your new year's meal.

Ingredients

2 medium or 3 small cucumbers (preferably of Kirby or English varieties), cut into chunks
1 green pepper, cored and cut into strips
1 red onion, cut into eight wedges
2-3 cups pomegranate juice
1 chunk (about 1 oz.) day-old bread
4 tablespoons olive oil
1 teaspoon salt
Juice of a lime
Sliced scallions, for garnish
Pomegranate seeds, for garnish

Process

In a food processor, chop the onion finely. Add the peppers, alternating with the cucumbers. Process until everything is chopped very, very fine. Add the bread and process until well-incorporated.

Then, with the food processor running on high speed, drizzle in the olive oil, then the lime juice. With the food processor still running, add 1 cup of the pomegranate juice. Stop processing and pour the gazpacho into a bowl. Depending on your preference of thickness, stir in the remaining 1 – 2 cups pomegranate juice. Chill for at least a half hour before serving. Serve garnished with pomegranate seeds and scallions and a drizzle of olive oil.

Quinoa Salad with Pomegranate, Orange & Watercress

Serves 6-8.

This salad gets its deeply refreshing pomegranate flavor from two additions: an abundance of pomegranate seeds and the reduced pomegranate juice – or pomegranate molasses – to the salad's dressing. Combined with the pepperiness of the watercress, sweetness of the citrus, and nuttiness of the quinoa and walnuts, this salad is a fresh, and quite addicting, addition to any Rosh Hashanah table.

Ingredients

- 1 cup brown quinoa
- 2 cups water
- 1 teaspoon kosher salt, plus more to taste
- 1 cup walnuts, chopped and toasted
- Seeds of two pomegranates
- 2 oranges
- 1 bunch watercress, stems removed
- 1 lemon
- 1 cup pomegranate juice, or ¼ cup pomegranate molasses
- ¼ cup extra virgin olive oil
- ½ teaspoon dried tarragon
- ½ teaspoon freshly ground black pepper

Process

Put the quinoa, water, and teaspoon of salt in a 4 quart saucepan and bring to a boil. Reduce to a simmer and cook, covered, for 15 minutes, or until all the water is absorbed. Let sit for 5 minutes and fluff with a fork.

Meanwhile, heat the pomegranate juice in a saucepan and heat to boiling. Boil for 10-15 minutes, or until reduced by three quarters. Take off heat and allow to cool.

Cut both ends of the oranges. Stand each orange on one cut end and slice the peel off the sides of the orange, removingas much of the white pith as possible without removing the flesh. Reserve segments. Then, slice between the membranes of the fruit to release the fruit's segments. Squeeze the membrane over a measuring cup to capture the juice and reserve. Mix the reserved orange juice with the juice of the lemon, reduced pomegranate juice, and olive oil. Add salt to taste, pepper, and tarragon. Whisk until emulsified.

Toss cooked quinoa with watercress leaves, orange segments, pomegranate seeds, and walnuts in a large salad bowl. Pour dressing over top and toss again.

Marisa's Pomegranate Jewelled Rice

Serves 8.

Rice is a key ingredient in both Sephardic and Spanish cooking. It receives the royal treatment in this recipe, crowned with a plethora of juicy pomegranate seeds. The color contrast of the red pomegranates on the white rice mirrors the complementary balance of flavors in this dish, with the garlic adding a savory counterpoint to the sweet fruit. Arranged on a large platter, it makes for an impressive centerpiece of your Rosh Hashanah meal as well as a delicious side dish.

Ingredients

2 cups long-grained rice, preferably jasmine
2 cups pomegranate seeds
3 tablespoons olive oil
1 onion, finely chopped
1 clove garlic, thinly sliced
½ inch piece of ginger, peeled and grated
½ tablespoon cinnamon

Process

Place the rice with 4 cups of cold water and a pinch of salt in a pot. Bring to a boil over medium heat then reduce to a simmer, covered, and let cook for 20 minutes. Without uncovering the pot, turn off the heat and let the rice stand for 5 minutes. Uncover and fluff with a fork.

Meanwhile, heat the olive oil over medium heat. Add the onions and cook for about 7 minutes, or until the onions start to take on a bit of color. Add the sliced garlic and cook the onion and the garlic for another 5-10 minutes, or until they are tinged brown. Add the ginger, and cook for 1 minute, until the ginger becomes aromatic.

Without lowering the heat, add the rice to the onion, garlic, and ginger. Cook, stirring constantly, for 2 minutes. Add the cinnamon and heat through another 1-2 minutes, or until the cinnamon releases its perfume. Remove the rice mixture from heat and let cool a few minutes. Add the pomegranate seeds and serve.

The Israeli Ambassador's Cauliflower

This recipe was given to one of our community members by the ex-ambassador of Israel to Spain, Alon Bar, after having been served it by the minister himself! Apparently, he grew up eating this dish on the kibbutz where he spent his childhood. Although the tahini is a traditional condiment on the Israeli table, the addition of the pomegranate seeds adds a original splash of tart brightness to the tahini's creamy bitterness, while also symbolizing the hope for abundance in the new year.

Ingredients

1 medium cauliflower, cut into florets
3 tablespoons olive oil
1 ½ teaspoons kosher salt
Juice of half a lemon
½ cup of tahini
1 clove of garlic, crushed

¼ - ½ cup cold water
½ cup chopped parsley
Seeds of 1 pomegranate

Process

Preheat the oven to 350°F. In a large bowl, mix the cauliflower florets with the olive oil and 1 teaspoon of the salt. Place the sheet in the oven and roast the cauliflower for 45 minutes, undisturbed.

Meanwhile, mix the tahini with the crushed garlic and salt. Add the lemon juice. Whisk in the water, using less if you'd like a sauce with a thicker consistency and more water if you'd like a more pourable sauce. You'll notice the color of the tahini change from very dark to quite light with the addition of the water.

After the cauliflower has roasted for 45 minutes, remove it from the oven and let it cool for 5 minutes. Then, place on a platter. Drizzle with the tahini sauce, reserving some to serve on the side. Sprinkle with the chopped parsley and pomegranate seeds.

Pomegranate Steak

Serves 2-4.

For me, the scent of this steak's marinade perfectly captures the warmth of what a holiday should be. The combination of the wine, pomegranate juice, spices, and garlic capture exactly the jumble of sweet and savory flavors that should adorn every holiday table, promising of the deliciousness to come. The marinade is then reduced while the steak cooks, becoming a rich sauce whose flavor, in addition to its fragrance, ensures the abundant new year's joy the pomegranate symbolizes.

Ingredients

1 lb. sirloin steaks, cut 1 ½" thick (any grilling steak will do – cooking time will vary)
1 teaspoon salt
½ freshly ground pepper
1 cup pomegranate juice
½ cup dry white or rose wine
Juice of 1 orange
½ teaspoon cumin
¼ teaspoon cinnamon
2 cloves garlic, crushed
1 bay leaf
2 tablespoons honey

Process

Place steaks in a wide, shallow dish. Season evenly with salt and pepper. In a bowl, whisk together the pomegranate juice, wine, orange juice, spices, and garlic. Pour mixture over steaks. Let the steaks marinate in the refrigerator for at least half an hour, preferably overnight.

Before cooking the steaks, remove them from the marinade. Pour the marinade in a saucepan and add the bay leaf and honey. Heat pan over medium-high heat and bring mixture to boil. Boil marinade for 20-30 minutes, or until very reduced and syrupy in consistency.

To cook the steaks, heat the grill or a grill pan over medium heat, waiting about 4-5 minutes until the pan or grill are very hot. Place the steaks on the grill or pan, cooking for 5 minutes on one side then flipping the steak and cooking on the opposite side for another 2-3 minutes for a steak cooked medium. Remove from heat and let rest, covered, for 5 minutes.

To serve, slice the steak in strips and serve drizzled with pomegranate reduction.

130 SQUASH

133 Italian Cream of Pumpkin Soup

135 Margarita's Squash Fritters

136 Marisa's Squash Empanadillas

138 Emanuele's Squash Galette

140 The Stayerman's Creamy Squash Soup

141 Ilana's Squash and Sage Pie

143 Roasted Squash with Walnut Arugula Sauce

According to the Jewish tradition, two important days open and seal judgment on each person: Rosh Hashanah, the new year, and Yom Kippur, the day of atonement. In the ten days between these two holidays, known as the Days of Awe, it is said that each person's fate for the coming year is written in the Book of Judgment – and so, in these ten days especially, each person is encouraged to be deeply introspective and repent before Yom Kippur. This relates to the symbolic ingredient of the squash because the Aramaic root of the word for squash, *kera*, is reminiscent of the Hebrew word *kara*, meaning "to read," as well as *karaa*, which means "to tear up." When we eat squash on Rosh Hashanah, we entreat that our bad judgment may be torn up and our good judgment read in the new year. The recipes in this section, though, demonstrate that even repentance can be delicious.

יְהִי רָצוֹן מִלְפָנֶיךָ ה' אֱלֹהֵינוּ וֵאלֹהֵי אֲבוֹתֵינוּ וְאִמּוֹתֵינוּ,
שֶׁתִּקְרַע רוֹעַ גְּזַר דִּינֵנוּ, וְיִקָּרְאוּ לְפָנֶיךָ זָכִיּוֹתֵינוּ

*Yehi ratzon milfanecha Adonai eloheinu v'elohei avoteinu v'imoteinu,
she'tikra roah gezeira dineinu, v'yikaru l'fanecha zakiyoteinu.*

May it be Your will, God and the God of our ancestors, that the evil of our verdicts be ripped, and that our merits be announced before you.

Italian Cream of Pumpkin Soup

Serves 8-10.

In both Spanish and Ladino, the word for squash – *calabaza* in Spanish and *kalavasa* in Ladino – can also mean pumpkin. This recipe offers a delectable way to introduce the pumpkin side of *kalavasa* into your Rosh Hashanah seder. During the fall in the northeastern United States, it's easy to find sweet sugar pumpkins, which cook up very nicely in this creamy pumpkin soup.

Ingredients

3 tablespoons olive oil
1 lb sugar pumpkin, cut into 1" chunks
2 medium carrots, peeled and cut into 1" pieces
2 large potatoes, peeled and cut into a large dice
1 large onion, chopped
1 teaspoon orange zest

2 teaspoons flour
1 teaspoon salt
1 cup water
1 ½ cups whole milk
Freshly ground pepper, to serve
Parmegiano Reggiano, grated, to garnish
Breadcrumbs, to garnish

Process

Heat the oil in a large heavy-bottomed pot. Add the pumpkin, carrots, potatoes, and onions. Cook for 5 minutes, until the pumpkin begins to soften. Add the water, orange zest, and salt and let cook on low heat until the carrots are fork tender, about 15 minutes. Add the flour and cook another 2 minutes.

Using an immersion blender, blend the vegetables together until they form a smooth, thick paste. Once blended, stir in the milk and let the puree simmer for 5 minutes on low heat, stirring frequently. To serve, ladle the puree into bowls. Top with the grated Parmigiano Reggiano, breadcrumbs, and a few grinds of fresh black pepper.

Margarita's Squash Fritters

Makes about 24 3-inch fritters.

Surprisingly delicate yet full-flavored, these squash fritters offer a novel, albeit simple, way to enjoy squash at its peak season. Roasting the squash, in this case butternut, concentrates the squash's flavor to almost-sweet; they make for an excellent blank palate to paint with toppings of all kinds. Here, we went with a topping of sour cream and tart-sweet dried cherries to accentuate the sweetness of the fritters, but you could just as easily – and deliciously – top the sour cream with chopped scallions and sprinkle of coarse sea salt for a more savory finish.

Ingredients

1 medium butternut squash, peeled and cubed
2/3 cup flour
2 eggs, beaten
½ teaspoon kosher salt
½ cup vegetable oil plus 2 tablespoons

Dried cherries and cranberries to garnish
Scallions

Process

Preheat the oven to 375°F. Place squash on a baking sheet and drizzle with the 2 tablespoons of vegetable oil. Roast in the oven 30 – 40 minutes, or until golden brown and mashable. Remove from oven and let cool.

Once the squash has cooled, mash it, being careful not to leave any lumps of squash. Add flour, eggs, and salt to the squash. The mixture should have the consistency of a thick batter. If the squash mixture is too thin, add more flour; too thick, add some water, tablespoon by tablespoon until you reach the desired consistency.

Heat ¼ cup of the vegetable oil in a skillet over medium heat. Once the oil is hot, drop the squash mixture by rounded tablespoon amounts in the pan. Lightly press each spoonful of batter in the pan to create a 2- to 3-inch round fritter. Fry on the first side for 3-5 minutes, until golden brown; flip onto the other side and cook for 3 more minutes, or until it's browned.

When its done, place each fritter on a paper-towel-lined plate to remove the excess oil. Serve warm with a dollop of sour cream and dried fruit or scallions, for a more savory fritter.

Marisa's Squash Empanadillas

Makes about 20 empanadillas.

Empanadas or *empanadillas* in the diminuitive, stuffed half-moons of oil-enriched dough, are a staple of the Spanish diet. They make for ideal midday or mid-morning snacks, packed into the lunches of schoolchildren or on the way to work with a *cafe con leche*. Instead of the traditional cheese or tuna, however, these pasties incorporate squash in their filling, making for a Rosh-Hashanah-appropriate twist on this Spanish classic.

Ingredients

1 lb squash (your preference – butternut or Delicata squash make delicious empanadillas), peeled, and cut into a medium dice
2 packages premade empanada wrappers (such as Goya brand) or make your own dough (recipe follows)
1 cup grated cheddar or gruyere
6 tablespoons olive oil
½ cup water
½ cup pumpkin seeds
½ teaspoon salt
Freshly ground pepper to taste
¼ teaspoon cayenne pepper (optional)

To prepare your own dough:

2 1/4 cups unbleached all-purpose flour, plus more for dusting
1 1/2 teaspoons salt
1 stick (1/2 cup) cold unsalted butter, cut into 1/2-inch cubes
1 large egg
1/3 cup ice water
1 tablespoon distilled white vinegar

If preparing your own dough:

Whisk together the flour and salt in a bowl. With your fingers, a fork, or a food processor, blend the butter into the flour mixture until it forms pea-sized lumps.

In another bowl, mix together the egg, ice water, and vinegar. Add this mixture to the flour and butter mixture, stirring to combine until it starts to form a coherent dough.

Turn the dough out onto a lightly floured surface. Knead lightly a few times with your hands, to ensure all ingredients are well incorporated. Flatten dough into a disk and let rest in the fridge for an hour.

Process

Heat 3 tablespoons of olive oil in a large skillet over medium heat. Once the oil is hot, add the squash and saute for 10 minutes. Add the water, salt, ground pepper, and cayenne pepper (if using). Cook another 10 minutes, or until all the water is absorbed and the squash is fork tender. Remove from heat.

Preheat the oven to 350°F. Prepare a baking sheet by brushing it with 1 tablespoon of olive oil.

If using homemade dough, remove the disk of dough 15 minutes before rolling out. Place disk of dough on a lightly floured surface and roll out to a 1/8 inch thickness. Using a 3" round cookie cutter, cut rounds of the dough.

To assemble the empanadas, take the store-bought of homemade rounds of dough and place a tablespoonful of filling in the middle of the circle. Top filling with a pinch of cheddar cheese. Fold one side of the round to the other and press closed with your fingers. Leave as is or crimp edges with a fork. Lightly brush the top of each empanada with the remaining olive oil and sprinkle with pumpkin seeds and/or leftover cheese.

Bake empanadillas for 15 minutes, or until golden brown.

Emanuele's Squash Galette

Serves 6-8.

Emanuele, who hails from Italy, explains that this squash galette is not necessarily a typical Rosh Hashanah dish, but rather a classic recipe from his mother Bruna's repertoire. He notes that *this recipe comes from my family, told from generation to generation, by word of mouth and through writing.* Although this recipe originally didn't have quantities attached to its ingredients, attesting to the personal touch and preference of each cook in Emanuele's family, we've attempted to most closely calibrate the correct measurements of each ingredient here. That being said, I encourage you to take a leaf from Emanuele's family's book and experiment with this recipe to discover the ideal squash galette for your family and holiday table.

Ingredients

For the dough:

1 cup flour
1/3 cup lukewarm water
½ teaspoon salt
¼ olive oil

For the filling:

3 tablespoons olive oil
1 pound butternut squash, peeled, cored, and cut into ½" chunks
1 onion, sliced
4 eggs
1 cup whole milk ricotta
1 teaspoon salt
½ cup grated parmesan
Freshly ground black pepper to taste

Process

To make the dough: In a large bowl, mix together the flour, the water, salt, and olive oil until it begins to stick together. Using your hand, lightly knead the mixture until it forms a fully incorporated ball of dough. Let rest for an hour in the refrigerator.

To make the filling: Heat the olive oil in a skillet over medium heat. Add the onion, and cook until it starts to brown, about 5 minutes. Add the squash and ½ teaspoon of salt. Cook the squash until it softens but retains its shape, about 10-15 minutes. Remove from heat.

In a large bowl, beat 3 of the eggs. Add the remaining salt, freshly ground black pepper to taste, grated parmesan, and ricotta. Add the cooked onions and squash and mix well.

To assemble the galette: Preheat the oven to 350°F. On a piece of parchment paper, roll the dough with a rolling pin lightly dusted with flour. Roll into a circle, about 12 to 13" in diameter, and about 1/8" thickness.

Place parchment-paper-lined dough on a baking sheet. Spoon squash mixture onto dough, being careful to leave the outer two edges of dough unfilled and piling the filling up towards the middle of the circle. Fold the edges an inch over the filling. Beat the remaining egg and brush it over the exposed edges of the dough.

Bake the galette for 30-40 minutes, or until the dough is golden brown and the filling has shrunk.

The Stayerman's Creamy Squash Soup

Serves 8-10.

Sara, who contributed this recipe, says that her mother would usually make this soup on cold days with toast and a layer of cheese melted atop the soup. Its comforting flavor is certainly warming, and would make a wonderful starter to a Rosh Hashanah meal on those years when the holiday falls more firmly in autumn. In a chilly season, this soup can serve as a reminder of the warmth that holiday celebrations can bring.

Ingredients

1 lb butternut squash, peeled and cut into a medium dice
2 large onions, separated and chopped
2 Italian peppers, separated and diced
1 clove garlic, minced
3 very ripe tomatoes, chopped
1 cup water
5 tablespoons olive oil
2 cubes vegetable bouillon
1 teaspoon salt
½ teaspoon freshly ground black pepper
½ teaspoon oregano
½ teaspoon dried basil
2 tablespoons butter
½ cup heavy cream

Process

In a large, heavy-bottomed pot, heat 3 tablespoons olive oil over medium heat. Sauté one onion, 1 of the peppers, and the garlic for about 5-7 minutes, until the onion becomes translucent. Add the tomatoes and sauté another 5 minutes. Add the water and the bouillon cubes. Add the oregano, basil, salt, and pepper. Bring to a boil and turn off the heat. Using an immersion blender, blend the mixture until smooth.

In another skillet, heat the remaining 2 tablespoons of olive oil and butter until the butter melts. Add the squash and sauté for a few minutes, stirring frequently. Add the previously made broth (above) and cream. Bring mixture to a boil and then lower heat and simmer for 20 minutes, stirring occasionally, until the squash is tender. Serve warm.

Ilana's Squash and Sage Pie

Serves 4.

Although the combination of sage and butternut squash is a usual pairing in the Northeastern United States, it's quite unusual to see this mixture in a Spanish dish. That being said, this pie offers a warming, quite comforting part of your holiday meal – one that will certainly add many merits to your Rosh Hashanah meal, as the blessing for the squash invites.

Ingredients

½ stick (4 tablespoons) unsalted butter
1 onion, thinly sliced
2 garlic cloves, minced
1 tablespoon minced fresh sage
1 teaspoon salt
Freshly ground black pepper, to taste
2 pound butternut squash, peeled and cut into 1/2-inch slices
3 tablespoons olive oil
1 17.3-oz box puff pastry (comes with 2 sheets)
¼ cup flour, to dust
8 oz gouda cheese, sliced or grated
1 egg, beaten

Process

Preheat the oven to 425°F. Lightly grease a 13" x 9" baking pan or Pyrex dish. In a large skillet, melt the butter. Add the onion, garlic, sage, ½ teaspoon salt, and pepper. Cook over medium heat, stirring occasionally, for 20-25 minutes. Once done cooking, take of the heat and reserve. Meanwhile, brush the slices of squash with the olive oil. Heat another skillet over medium-high heat. Sear the squash, 2-3 minutes on each side, until softened. Sprinkle with the remaining ½ teaspoon of salt. Once cooked, reserve pieces of squash on a plate.

Once the vegetables are cooked, dust a working surface with the flour. Place one sheet of the puff pastry on the work surface and roll it out, until it can cover the bottom of the baking pan. Repeat with the other sheet. Mold one of the sheets of puff pastry to the baking pan. Cover it with tin foil and pour beans or pie weights in the pan. Bake the dough, about 5 minutes, or until it begins to puff but does not shrink back from the pan.

Take the pre-baked dough out of the oven. Working in layers, spread a thin layer of the onion mixture on the bottom of the dough, then place pieces of squash in a single layer atop the onion mixture. Top with a thin layer of gouda cheese. Repeat two to three times, alternating layers of onion mixture, squash, and cheese. Place the other sheet of puff pastry atop the filling and pinch it to the pre-baked puff pastry to seal the filling within the pastry. Poke the top of the puff pastry with a fork and brush with the eggwash. Bake the pie for 10-15 minutes, or until it turns golden brown and begins to puff up.

Roasted Squash with Arugula-Walnut Sauce

Serves 4.

This dish offers an inventive way of enjoying the best of late summer and early fall produce. While the squash roasts, you can whip up the delightful arugula-walnut sauce that's reminiscent of pesto in its garlicky, slightly herbaceous flavor. The pairing turns out to be a match made in heaven – the slight sweetness of the squash mellowing out the verdant bitterness of the sauce – and an apt metaphor for the nature of the transition from the old year to the new.

Ingredients

2 pound butternut squash, peeled, de-seeded, and cut into ½" thick slices
2/3 cup plus 3 tablespoons olive oil
1 teaspoon salt
½ teaspoon freshly ground black pepper
½ cup walnuts
1 shallot, skin removed and sliced in half

1 clove garlic
2 cups arugula leaves, plus more for serving
Juice of 1 lemon
3 – 5 tablespoons water

Process

Preheat oven to 375°F. Lay squash slices on a baking sheet and brush with 3 tablespoons of olive oil. Sprinkle with ½ teaspoon of salt and a pinch of black pepper. Roast for 20-25 minutes, flipping the slices once halfway through. Once fork tender, remove the squash from the oven and let cool 5 minutes.

Meanwhile, in a food processor, finely chop the shallot and garlic. Add the walnuts and process until finely ground. Add the two cups of arugula and process until finely chopped. With the food processor running, add the remaining salt and black pepper, then the lemon juice. Process another minute. Then, with the processor still running, gradually drizzle in the olive oil until the color of the mixture is lightened and the mixture's consistency has thinned. Add the water, 1 tablespoon at a time, until the mixture has loosened enough to pour.

Place the extra arugula on a plate or a large, shallow dish. Arrange the squash slices on top and drizzle with the arugula-walnut sauce.

Menus

Making a holiday meal requires a huge amount of forethought and planning to execute. Whether you're in need of inspiration or short on prep time, we've come up with a variety of menus you ca[n] use for your Rosh Hashanah meal. In each of these menus, we've attempted to represent each siman, organized according to a men[u] theme. Where you find that not all the simanim are included, it'[s] because we felt it disrupted the coherent flow of the menu.

Each of these menus reflects the different ways you can incorpora[te] the dishes you find in this book within your Rosh Hashanah celebration.

May they inspire you and help you invite blessings into the new ye[ar]. ¡Buen aprovecho! (Bon appetit!)

Autumn Seasonal

•

Margarita's Beet and Apple Salad
Honey Chicken
(if you're not serving a kosher menu;
omit should you want a dairy meal)
Roasted Leeks with Goat Cheese and Balsamic
Reduction

• •

Marisa's Jewelled Rice
Ilana's Squash and Sage Pie
Yael's Sabbath Cod Fritters

• • •

Zohar's White Beans with Honey
Date Walnut Pie
Classic Apple Crumble

Summer Seasonal

·

Svekol'nik
Fried Eggplant with Date Syrup
Green Beans Esparragados

· ·

Honeyed Turnips
Noa's Leek Salad
Roasted Squash with Arugula-Walnut Sauce
Orange Salmon

· · ·

Apple Strudel

Spanish

•

Pomegranate Gazpacho
Adele's Leek Crema
Marisa's Squash Empanadillas
Salad Olivier, or Ensaladilla Rusa
Margarita's Beet and Apple Salad

• •

Dani's Cocido
(if you're not serving a kosher menu;
omit should you want a dairy meal)
Ceutan Fish (Fish with Pipirrana)

• • •

Yael's Honey Cigars
Date Pudding Cake

Sweet Seder

•

Beet Waldorf Salad
Roasted Leeks with Balsamic Reduction and Goat Cheese
Quinoa Salad with Pomegranate, Orange, and Watercress
Margarita's Squash Fritters

• •

Zohar's White Beans with Honey
Duck Breast with Apples, Cranberries & Mint
Soy-Silan Salmon
(if you're not serving a kosher menu;
omit should you want a dairy meal)

• • •

Date Truffles
Turkish Poppy Seed Cake

Ottoman Sephardic

•

The Stayerman's Creamy Squash Soup
Turkish Bean Salad
Margarita's Beet and Apple Salad
Leek Kofte

• •

Borekas de Prasa
The Ambassador's Cauliflower with
Tahini & Pomegranate
Ilana's Date, Apricot, Rice Salad
Soy-Silan Salmon

• • •

Apple Strudel
Turkish Poppy Seed Cake

Comunidad Special

•

Alicia's Challah
Salad Olivier, or Ensaladilla Rusa
Meme's Beet and Apple Salad

• •

Guefilte Fish
Pasta with Leek Sauce and Salmon
Emanuele's Squash Galette
Marisa's Jewelled Rice
Leidy's Beans with Ground Beef

• • •

Date Truffles

Mediterranean

•

Green Beans Esparragados
Margarita's Beet and Apple Salad

• •

Ceutan Fish (Fish with Pipirrana)
Pasta with Leek Sauce and Salmon
The Ambassador's Cauliflower with Tahini & Pomegranate
Italian Cream of Pumpkin Soup

• • •

Silka's Apple Cake
Yael's Honey Cigars
Date Pudding Cake

Ashkenazi-inspired

•

Alicia's Challah
The Stayermans' Borscht
Ilana's Tsimmes
Margarita's Squash Fritters

• •

Zohar's White Beans with Honey
Roasted Leeks with Balsamic Reduction
and Goat Cheese
(omit the cheese should you be serving a meat meal)
Guefilte Fish
Pomegranate Steak

• • •

Date Walnut Pie

Israeli-inspired

•

Middle Eastern Carrot Salad
Beet Waldorf Salad
Turkish Bean Salad

• •

Forshmak
Noa's Leek Salad
The Ambassador's Cauliflower with Tahini &
Pomegranate
Roasted Squash with Walnut-Arugula Sauce

• • •

Silka's Apple Cake
Yael's Honey Cigars

Hors D'Oeuvres

•

Pomegranate Gazpacho
Salad Olivier, or Ensaladilla Rusa
Turkish Bean Salad

• •

Beet and Lentil "Burgers"
Yael's Sabbath Cod Fritters
Marisa's Squash Empanadillas
Borekas de Prasa

• • •

Date Truffles
Yael's Honey Cigars

About the Organizing Committee

About the Editor

Sara M. Gardner is a food historian and researcher specializing in the culinary heritage and cultural identity of the Sephardic Jews. She currently works as the Associate Director for Young Adult Programs at Hebrew College, a rabbinical school located in Newton, MA. Before coming to Hebrew College, Sara conducted research on the culinary heritage and cultural identity of Sephardic Jews in Madrid as a Fulbright Scholar. Sara is also the creator and head blogger of Boka Dulse (www.bokadulse.com), a food blog dedicated to Jewish food history, and regularly contributes Jewish food history content to various Jewish media platforms, including The Nosher and RadioSefarad. An avid cook and food historian, Sara also teaches cooking classes – some of her past teaching engagements include the Reform Jewish Community of Madrid and The Gefilteria. In 2016, Sara graduated with a BA in International Literary & Visual Studies and Spanish from Tufts University. This is her first cookbook.

About the Project Manager

Yael Cobano was born in a small multicultural Spanish city on the north coast of Africa, and is founder and President of the Reform Jewish Community of Madrid. She holds University studies in Law and International Conflict Resolution. She has been trained by seminars of the Union for Reform Judaism (URJ), Reform Judaism UK, Joint Distribution Committee (JDC) and European Council of Jewish Communities (ECJC) in different aspects such as Jewish education, liturgy and security. She has been Chair of and speaker at different sessions in the WUPJ, URJ and EUPJ conferences. Yael is currently a Rabbinic student of Iberoamerican Institute for Reform Rabbinical Education (WUPJ-WUPJ-Amlat). Her passions are knowledge, social action, food and literature.

About the Designer / Illustrator

Participating in this project from Israel is Maya Bank, graphic artist graduated from the Escuela Superior de Diseño de Madrid in graphic and product design. She has been awarded the second prize of the Rijksstudio Contest by The National Museum of Holland, Rijksmuseum. Her work has been exhibited in the Museo della Carta e della Filigrana, Fabriano (Italy), the Biblioteca Nacional de España and DIMAD-Matadero, Madrid (Spain).

About the Organizing Committee Chair

Margarita Gokun Silver is a freelance writer and an artist. Her work has appeared in The New York Times, The Washington Post, The Wall Street Journal, BBC, NPR, The Atlantic, The Forward, Hadassah Magazine, and Haaretz, among others. Her art has been exhibited in the US and Spain. She is a dual resident of Madrid, Spain and Athens, Greece.

Made in United States
Orlando, FL
12 March 2024